Writers of Wales

R. S. Thomas

Writers of Wales

R. S. Thomas

Tony Brown

University of Wales Press

Cardiff 2006

© Tony Brown, 2006

Reprinted 2009

British Library Cataloguing-in-Publication Data.
A catalogue record for this book is available from the British Library.

ISBN 978-0-7083-1800-3

Printed in Wales by Dinefwr Press, Llandybïe *www.dinefwrpress.co.uk*

For Nancy, Sara and Alys

There was a hope
he was outside of, with no-one
to ask him in [. . .]

R. S. Thomas, *The Echoes Return Slow*

Contents

Illustrations between pages 118–119

Acknowledgements

Conversations, over numerous years, about R. S. Thomas and his work, with fellow scholars, undergraduate and postgraduate students, and visitors to the R. S. Thomas Study Centre at University of Wales, Bangor, mean that my debts are many and varied. But in particular I am grateful for discussion in recent years with my Co-director at the Centre, Dr Jason Walford Davies, and with my friend and colleague, Professor M. Wynn Thomas (University of Wales Swansea), who is also the poet's literary executor. My thinking about Thomas's personality and his references to his own insecurity of identity has been focussed by conversation with Dr Barbara Prys-Williams, and my indebtedness to her work on *The Echoes Return Slow* will be evident in the text. Discussion with postgraduate students working in the field is perhaps the best possible way of keeping one's ideas sharp and thinking further; I have been fortunate to have had working with me at the Centre at Bangor some especially able students of R. S. Thomas's writing: Dr Fflur Dafydd, Daniel Westover and Sam Perry (University of Leicester). The poet's son, Mr Gwydion Thomas has been unfailingly supportive and I am especially grateful to him for permission to publish several photographs of his father, as well as permission to quote extensively from R. S. Thomas's writing and broadcasts. Dr T. Robin Chapman generously drew my attention to relevant material during his own research on Islwyn Ffowc Elis. I am grateful to colleagues at the University of Wales Press, especially Sarah Lewis, for their expertise – and for their patience in the over-long gestation of the present work. The series editor, Professor Meic Stephens, made many helpful suggestions on the text and saved me from a number of errors; those that remain are of course my own responsibility. Mrs Linda Jones, Research Co-ordinator in the Department of English at Bangor has, as ever, been indispensable in the preparation of text.

I am grateful to Mrs Eirlys Ffowc Elis for permission to quote from unpublished writing by her late husband, Islwyn Ffowc Elis; to the BBC in Cardiff and London for permission to quote from unpublished broadcasts by R. S. Thomas; to the late Mr Ian Cameron, a cousin of the poet, for permission to publish the photograph of R. S. and Elsi Thomas in 1940; to members of St Mary Magdelane's Church, Tallarn Green, for giving me a copy of the photograph of R. S. and Elsi Thomas taken when he was a curate there (and for a memorable evening talking about the poet in the little church where he once served).

Abbreviations

Chapter I
From Holyhead to Manafon

Those Others

A gofid gwerin gyfan
Yn fy nghri fel taerni tân
　　　　　Dewi Emrys

I have looked long at this land,
Trying to understand
My place in it—why,
With each fertile country
So free of its room,
This was the cramped womb
At last took me in
From the void of unbeing.

Hate takes a long time
To grow in, and mine
Has increased from birth;
Not for the brute earth
That is strong here and clean
And plain in its meaning
As none of the books are
That tell but of the war

Of heart and head, leaving
The wild birds to sing
The best songs; I find
This hate's for my own kind,
For men of the Welsh race
Who brood with dark face
Over their thin navel
To learn what to sell;

> Yet not for them all either,
> There are still those other
> Castaways on a sea
> Of grass, who call to me,
> Clinging to their doomed farms;
> Their hearts though rough are warm
> And firm, and their slow wake
> Through time bleeds for our sake. (*T* 31–2)

'Those Others' was published in 1961, by which time R. S. Thomas had left Manafon, the first parish where he had served as priest, and left the hills of Montgomeryshire, the landscape of the poems which had established his reputation as a poet in the 1950s. He was now vicar at St Michael's, Eglwys-fach, not far from Aberystwyth. In many ways it is a poem in which the poet takes stock of his situation. It anticipates the political polarities of much of the work which was to follow in the 1960s: Thomas's vigorous distaste, amounting to hatred, for those who were willing to market Wales as a commodity for tourists, to sell Wales, its natural beauty, its history and its culture to tourists from England, and his assertion of the need for stubborn resistance to the intrusive world of consumerism and market values which he saw such tourism as representing. For an emblem of that resistance, of another, truer way of life, the poet looks back, as he does so often in the poetry of the 1960s, to the beleaguered hill farmers of Montgomeryshire, the last remnants of what Thomas sees as an older, truer way of life, rooted in the rhythms of Welsh rural life.

The epigraph from Dewi Emrys, added to the poem when it was collected in *Tares* (1961), focuses the cultural struggle that the poem engages: 'With the pain of a whole people / In my cry like the fervency of fire'. As Jason Walford Davies has recently pointed out, Dewi Emrys's poem, 'Yr Alltud' ('The Exile'), published in the 1940s, concerns a Welshman forced abroad for avenging the theft of his family's land; the poem vividly evokes the doomed farms, the displacement of the native hill farmers and the inexorable destruction of a whole way of life.[1] Thomas himself had seen the evidence of that displacement, the ruins of the abandoned farms, as he had walked the hills of Montgomeryshire. But this is not the only personal element in the poem, and not perhaps the only resonance that Dewi Emrys's poem has. For 'Those Others' is an autobiographical, as well as a cultural, taking stock, though the two are manifestly deeply intermeshed. For if Dewi Emrys's poem gives voice to an exile, Thomas's poem begins with the experience of being brought inside ('took me in'), of being born, or reborn, into a new identity, associated with the authentic life of the earth and emblematized by the life of the hill farmers. Their way of life, in other words, has deeply personal, not just cultural, resonance for the poet: they are rooted in a place, and know the truth of who they are. (In the poem's original version, their hearts are 'Warm / And true'.)

This is not to say, though, that 'Those Others' indicates that the sense of identity into which the poet feels he has been reborn is a secure one; indeed the image given of the hill farmers' 'clinging' to the place where they belong, suggests the contrary and we are aware anyway of the poet's isolated distance from them (they 'call to me'). What one senses, in fact, is not an escape from the 'void of unbeing' into an assured sense of self but an underlying awareness of continued vulnerability. In *The Echoes Return Slow*, an autobiographical sequence that is by turn revealing and deeply enigmatic, Thomas, writing of his period at Eglwys-fach, recalls

> An obsession with nothing
> distinguished him from his co-
> thinkers. [. . .]
> > It was
> a mental property, inherited
> on his coming of age; the
> recessive thought that,
> when progress is about
> to be guaranteed, returns one
> to the void. (*ERS* 49)

Barbara Prys-Williams, in seeking to analyse the personal tensions in *Echoes*, argues that Thomas appears to be someone with 'a weak sense of self' and she comments on how at some points in the sequence 'he embodies the very nebulousness he is experiencing in the self by allowing the poem itself to drift spatially':

> In a dissolving
> world what certainties
> for the self, whose identity
> is its performance? (ERS 33)[2]

The notion of identity as something which we perform rather than securely inhabit, in a contemporary world lacking the shared social and cultural values which in previous generations made individual identity less problematic, is scarcely unique to R. S. Thomas, but he seems to have experienced this insecurity of identity with particular acuteness: 'Certainly it has come to me many times with a catch in the breath that I don't know who I am', he writes in an autobiographical essay.[3] The very title of his autobiography, *Neb* ('Nobody', or 'Anybody'), is symptomatic of this same insecurity and there are in the book moments when Thomas recalls similar disturbing episodes in which the every-day sense of self is disrupted in a moment that is a kind of negative epiphany:

> [T]here was something unreal about his attempts to take part in college activities. [. . .] 'Who does he think he is?' was the murmur he would hear from time to time. But he didn't know who he was. He was no-one. Sometimes during a dance he would go outside and look through the windows at the merry crowd inside, and see it all as something unreal. (A 38)

It is a scene, one might argue, that is emblematic of R. S. Thomas's relation to the life in which he has found himself: detached, looking on, or looking in from outside, aware of himself as an outsider, deracinated, and seeking some sense of involvement in a way of life which would give him a sense of belonging, a place which would allow him to *be*, to realize himself fully, emotionally, imaginatively and spiritually, a place which would give him a sense of home. It is a longing which haunts Thomas's writing, from the attempt to locate himself within Welsh culture –

> I can't speak my own
> Language—Iesu,
> All those good words;
> And I outside them. ('Welsh', *BT* 15)

– to the long struggle to end his spiritual aloneness and feel himself at one with the 'ultimate reality', which is God:

> There was a hope
> he was outside of, with no-one
> to ask him in. (*ERS* 49)

The process of seeking a new sense of belonging to which Thomas looks back in 'Those Others' ostensibly has its beginning when, during his time as a curate at Tallarn Green in the parish of Hanmer, Flintshire (1940–2), Thomas looked westward:

And from there, some fifteen miles away, I saw at dusk the hills of Wales rising, telling as before of enchanting and mysterious things. I realised what I had done. That was not my place, on the plain amongst Welshmen with English accents and attitudes. I set about learning Welsh, in order to be able to return to the true Wales of my imagination. (*A* 10)

That last, richly ambiguous phrase is of course a crucial one; his construction of the 'Wales' to which he was to 'return' was to be a deeply personal one, born of his own emotional and imaginative needs. It is evident that the years of Thomas's curacy first at Chirk (1937–40) and then at Hanmer (1940–2) were years of emotional unease and restlessness. In part this was to be expected: a young man, fresh from theological college and in an unfamiliar area, confronting for the first time the emotional and spiritual demands of ministering to ordinary parishioners, people in spiritual crisis or, more often, facing serious illness ('It was here, for the first time, that he came face to face with the problem of pain', *A* 43). But there seem also to have been other tensions: as the international political situation darkened in the late 1930s, the young curate was reading the work of Hewlett Johnson, the 'Red Dean' of Canterbury, and he sympathized with Johnson's view that much of the blame for the European crisis could be laid at the feet of international capitalism. In a letter accompanying some poems sent at this time to the recently-founded *Welsh Review*, Thomas tells the editor, 'As a clergyman I am naturally of a pacifist and rather 'Left' tendency and cannot think that the long trail of guilt leads back to one person or government only.'[4] But such views were not popular and his vicar quickly instructed him not to 'preach such stuff'. As Thomas notes in his autobiography, 'It was this that opened his eyes to a fact of which he would later become more and more aware: the Church was not willing to condemn war, only to exhort young men to do their "duty" then pray for them'; to him it was clear that Christ was a pacifist, 'but not so the Church established in his name' (*A* 44). It was only after the war that Thomas was publicly critical of the Church in Wales, attacking its lack of opposition to militarism as well as its lack of leadership in matters of Welsh national identity.[5] But such conflicts in belief must have caused the young curate to reflect deeply on the values of the Church in which he had just begun to serve and on the nature of his role within it, adding to his unease at Chirk.

It was an unease which ultimately amounted to what might, in existentialist terms, be defined as a sense of inauthenticity, the sense, again, of not being in secure possession of one's own identity, of who one is, being instead defined and 'moulded by external influences, whether these be circumstances, moral codes, political or ecclesiastical authorities'.[6] Or, one might add, domestic or familial influence. In a revealing late poem Thomas writes:

> How old was he, when he asked
> who he was, and receiving

       no answer, asked who they
       were, who projected images
       of themselves on an unwilling
       audience. They named him, adding
       the preliminary politeness, endorsing
       a claim to gentility he did not
       possess. The advance towards Christian
       terms was to an understanding of the significance
       of repentance, courtesy put under greater
       constraint; an effort to sustain the role
       they insisted that he had written.
       Who reaches such straits flees
       to the sanctuary of his mirror for re-assurance
       that he is still there, challenging the eyes
       to look back into his own and not
       at the third person over his shoulder. ('Roles', *EA* 12)

While this is a poem from the 1980s, it looks back precisely to issues that it seems likely Thomas was confronting at Chirk about the choice of life he had made: how real had been that choice, and thus how authentic was his present life? The resort to the mirror for reassurance of identity at a time of self-alienation and self-questioning is a motif that is revealingly recurrent throughout Thomas's work; in a perceptive examination of this motif, Katie Gramich has recently related it to allusions to the myth of Narcissus and pointed out that psychoanalytic theorists have suggested that what has been called 'negative narcissism' can be related to 'anxious self-dissatisfaction' and internalized resentment against parental strictures.[7] As Gramich points out, Thomas's relationship with his mother, to judge from his various comments about her, was a complex one: 'she was the boss. My father being much of the time at sea, it was to her I was answerable' (*MS* 3). Clearly, her only child was, especially in the father's absence, the focus of Margaret Thomas's affection, and emotional needs: the night before he left home in Holyhead for University in Bangor, he awoke to find his mother desperately 'kissing him over and over' (*A* 36). Clearly in such a relationship, the mother's views about her son's future career are going to have considerable influence, especially when the son seems to have had no clear ambitions of his own: 'My mother, early orphaned and brought up by a half-brother who was a vicar, fancied the Church. Shy as I was, I offered no resistance' (*MS* 3). The son went to Bangor to study Classics on a Church in Wales scholarship and, acutely aware of financial pressures at home – his father's increasing deafness meant that he could no longer go to sea – Thomas worked single-mindedly at his studies in order to graduate. After only a year's theological study at St Michael's College in Llandaff, Cardiff, instead of the usual two, he was ordained and took up his post at Chirk. It was perhaps not surprising that it was only then, facing the challenges of his ministry, that he begins to question the nature and values of the life he was now living.

Manifestly many of those values also had their roots in his upbringing as his mother's son. Brought up herself as a child of the vicarage, Margaret Thomas clearly sought to run a home which conformed carefully to ideals of bourgeois respectability, whatever the financial realities ('endorsing / a claim to gentility he did not / possess'); as a young child Thomas had been sent 'to some kind of school where the "nice" people of the town sent their children' (*A* 29) and as he grew up it seems likely that it was his mother who ensured that he 'moved in refined circles' (*A* 36). Those circles were like his own home and education, English-speaking. For this generation English was the language of social advancement, Welsh the badge of the uncultured and backward-looking. Thus R. S. Thomas's decision at Tallarn Green to learn Welsh in order to return to the 'true Wales' of his imagination represents a rejection of the values of his upbringing, a rejection born of his growing sense of inauthenticity, his increasing scepticism towards the conformism of English bourgeois respectability and the identity it had created for him. But such rejection is not easily achieved; in the uncollected 'Autobiography' Thomas writes that he had studied:

> to become the rat
> that will desert
> the foundering vessel
> of their pride; but home
> is a long time sinking. All
> my life I must swim
> out of the suction of its vortex.[8]

The guilt is as clear as the determined struggle (the poem was published in the year of Margaret Thomas's death) while the vehemence of expression is a measure of the depth of feeling. The speaker of 'Welsh' (*BT* 15) asserts that he is 'a real Cymro', but is unable to speak Welsh. One cannot simplistically identify the speaker with the poet ('I'm Welsh, see' hardly sounds like R. S. Thomas) but 'She claimed me, / Brought me up nice, / No hardship' suggests the reason why the narrator cannot speak Welsh; the poem ends:

> I want the town, even
> The open door
> Framing a slut,
> So she can speak Welsh
> And bear children
> To accuse the womb
> That bore me.

Not only is maternal culpability asserted but the vigour of the expression, the vehemence of the register, as well as the affirmation itself represent an overt affront to bourgeois gentility.

Thomas's sailor father, on the other hand, is repeatedly seen as a heroic figure, the bold navigator of the world's oceans, finally inveigled home by wife and familial duty to a more humdrum life on the Irish ferries:

> Was he aware
> of a vicarage garden
> that was the cramped harbour
> he came to?

> [. . .] The deep
> sea and the old call
> to abandon it
> for the narrow channel
> from her and back. The chair
> was waiting and the slippers
> by the soft fire
> that would destroy him. ('Salt', *LP* 159–63)

The sad figure of his father – 'a ship's captain / with no crew, a navigator / without a port' – becomes a poignant warning to the poet of the dangers of the threat to selfhood, especially male selfhood, of the domestic – 'I take his failure / for ensign'. Indeed 'domestication' becomes a powerful pejorative term for Thomas, applied to all those human systems and processes which seek to control the vitality of natural life, reduce it to the inert and mechanical; the natural world is a 'kind of symbol of God over against the domesticating urge in man. [. . .] The aircraft, the motors [. . .] rending the silence. [. . .] The wild, places are becoming domesticated' (*MS* 19, 35). In 'Young and Old', the aircraft attempt to 'Domesticate the huge sky' (*YO* 7).

At Chirk Thomas's restlessness, his sense of alienation, manifested itself in a longing for a way of life the values of which were simpler, more fulfilling, more authentic, values which he began to associate with the land to the west; not with his memories of bourgeois life in Holyhead, of course, but with a way of life Thomas felt he glimpsed in Yeats's early writing, in poetry and in prose such as *The Celtic Twilight* (1893), about Celtic Ireland, of a simple peasant culture where identity, both communal and individual, was unproblematic, growing from a rich imaginative heritage, rooted in a particular place. Thomas's *'hiraeth* for the west' (*A* 45) found another source when he came upon the fanciful popular romantic fiction, set in the Gaelic-speaking Hebrides, that William Sharp (1855–1905) had published in the 1890s under the pen name of 'Fiona Macleod'. There, in novels like *The Mountain Lovers* (1895) and, especially, *Pharais* (1893) Thomas found an expression of 'the Celtic joy in the life of nature – the Celtic vision',[9] tales of simple peasant life, set against powerful evocations of the natural landscape and dynamic windswept shores. Macleod, along with Yeats, came to represent 'exactly the life that he would love to live among the peat and the heather on the west coast' (*A* 45). It is clearly a measure of that longing, and thus of his own inner discontent, that he set off to visit the Scottish islands with his fiancée, the artist Mildred Eldridge, in the summer of 1937; the weather was bad and he found none of the romantic peasant life he had found in the pages of Macleod's fiction. But this seems to have done little to damage Thomas's vision of Celtic life and the following year found him in Ireland visiting Seamus O'Sullivan, editor of *The Dublin Magazine*, then heading west to Galway. Here he finally experienced something of the magical life he had been seeking:

> The young man had noticed the number of carts that stood on the square in Galway, having come there with a load of seaweed, and as night began to fall, he was passed by cart after cart on its way home to the west. As each cart passed him the driver greeted him in Irish. This, and the smell of the peat in his nostrils, raised his spirits and filled him with new hope. (*A* 47)

Marriage to Mildred Eldridge (known as 'Elsi') in 1940 – they attempted to get a harpist to play after the wedding, as at a *neithior*, a traditional Welsh marriage-feast (*A* 49) – and the subsequent move to Tallarn Green seem to have done little to ease Thomas's sense of discontent; in a later essay he writes of his 'two terrible years' at Tallarn Green. The early poem 'Hiraeth' (*SF* 34) seems, from its reference to his 'leafless house [. . .] upon the plain', to date from those years and thus the longing expressed in the poem can be seen not just as nostalgia for the shores of his native Anglesey from his current situation 'Far inland, far inland', but for a life and an environment that is free, natural and, in the reference to Ceridwen's bowl, emblematic of the potential for rebirth:

> And in the glitter of stars, shoal upon shoal,
> Thicker than bubbles in Ceridwen's bowl,
> The running of the sea under the wind,
> Rough with silver, comes before my mind. (*SF* 34)

Meanwhile German bombers droned nightly over the area, heading for the docks of Merseyside, occasionally off-loading bombs in the fields nearby. Thomas's internal tensions were manifestly exacerbated by the coming of war. It was a stress, though, that was not only the result of external danger, but, again, of Thomas's own inner divisions. As a pacifist priest he viewed with horror the carnage and destruction that had been loosed upon the world. At the same time, however, it is evident that, for all the sincerity of his pacifist beliefs, a mind as scrupulous as Thomas's could not at the same time avoid examining and questioning his own motives, aware that:

> Others were brave. Whether volunteering or conscripted, they went forth to the war, as their fellows had done hundreds of years. [. . .] What does a man do with his silence, his aloneness, but suffer the sapping of unanswerable questions? (*ERS* 20)

Even writing decades later, Thomas reconstructs the period explicitly in terms of a divided self, caught once more uncertainly, and guiltily, between that which is authentic but socially inglorious and the role he might play:

> Entered for life, failing
> to qualify; understudied
> for his persona, became identical
> with his twin. Confronted
> as the other, knew credit
> was his or the triumph
> of an imposture. [. . .]
> When volunteers
> were called for to play
> death's part, stood modestly
> in the wings, preferring rather
> to be prompter than prompted. (*ERS* 21)

Thus the 'true Wales' which Thomas imaginatively constructs as he looks westward from Tallarn Green is ultimately a version of the simple Celtic life, free both of external danger and internal tension, a life and community in which he can begin to *belong*, develop an authentic self. The prose passage in *The Echoes Return Slow* which recalls his move to mid-Wales, on his appointment as rector of Manafon, Montgomeryshire, opens with a sense of tranquil relief:

> What had been blue shadows on a longed-for horizon, traced on an inherited background, were shown in time to contain this valley, this village and a church built with stones from the river, where the rectory stood, plangent as a mahogany piano. The stream was a bright tuning fork in the moonlight. (*ERS* 24)

But the passage ends more bleakly (and with a fascinating echo of 'Hiraeth' written so many years earlier): 'The young man was sent unprepared to expose his ignorance of life in a leafless pulpit.' R. S. Thomas wrote on several occasions of the impact upon him of arriving in his new agricultural parish:

> I came out of a kind of bourgeois environment which, especially in modern times, is protected; it's cushioned from some of the harsher realities; and this muck and blood and hardness, the rain and the spittle and the phlegm of farm life was, of course, a shock to begin with and one felt that this was something not quite part of the order of things.[10]

This was far from being the idyllic, simple peasant life of the Celtic west:

> I now found myself amongst tough, materialistic, hard-working people, who measured one another by the acre and by the pound; Welshmen who had turned their backs on their cultural inheritance and gone to trade in Welshpool and Oswestry and Shrewsbury. (*A* 11)

While the parish was not Welsh-speaking, there were Welsh speakers in the surrounding hill communities and a chapel on the edge of the moorland where there were services and *eisteddfodau* in Welsh and there, with the minister, Thomas continued slowly to learn the Welsh language.

But as he walked the moorland above Manafon, he found not a thriving community but everywhere evidence of economic decay and dereliction; farm houses which from a distance he imagined to be inhabited by 'some poetically-minded hill farmer in love with solitude, with a kitchen that might prove the perfect setting for a *noson lawen'* ('The Depopulation of the Welsh Hill Country', *SP* 18) turned out, as he got closer, to be uninhabited and in ruins. This was not just a matter of economic decline but, as Thomas argued in the pages of Keidrych Rhys's *Wales*, the uprooting and destruction of a culture; those whom economic pressures were forcing from the land 'were losing for ever their real meaning in life' (*SP* 18), joining the modern world of the *déracinés*. The irony for Thomas was profound: here he felt *had* been a Welsh communal life as rich as that he had found in the pages of Yeats and Macleod and had glimpsed in Galway. But its last traces had all but slipped away before he could make contact with it; as he walked the empty hills he was, almost emblematically, still a lone outsider:

> When I am there, I hear the curlew mourning the people who have passed away, and I dream of the days that were, the days of *Calan Mai* and the hafoty; days when the Welsh went to the high pastures to live for a season at least, 'At the bright hem of God / In the heather, in the heather'. Time stands still in these areas, and it is easy to forget the contemporary world. After a day in them, I return to my house in the valley like a stranger.[11]

Calan Mai, May Day, was traditionally when the farming community had moved with their flocks from the *hendre*, the 'old settlement' in the valley, to the hill pastures where they spent the summer in the *hafoty*, the summer house. Yeats' and Macleod's peasant cultures – in so far as they had ever existed in quite the form in which these writers portrayed them – had disappeared in the nineteenth century, and it is similarly a matter for speculation whether the hill pastures of Wales had ever been the sun-filled site of a rich imaginative culture, with the shepherds and their families 'swapping *englynion* over the peat cutting' ('The Mountains', *SP* 82). But it is clearly a myth, a personal myth, of simple, non-bourgeois communal life that had profound significance for Thomas, and in his writing in the early years at Manafon he still determinedly detects its last remnants amongst the hill farmers and their families: 'The fact is that despite the many ruined homesteads in these upland districts, there are others still managing to hold out [. . .] These are the true Welsh peasantry and to know them is to feel a real affection for them', albeit 'these same people are but the shadows of what their fathers were' (*SP* 19–20); these, of course, are 'those others' who, by 1961, when Thomas looks back from Eglwys-fach, are the beleaguered essence of authentic Wales.

Thomas had continued to write poetry during his years at Chirk and Tallarn Green, but as yet the Modernism of Eliot and Pound was unknown to him; indeed his poetry had scarcely advanced from the lyrics of romantic, rural loneliness that he had been writing as a student at Bangor: 'I was [. . .] a confirmed open-air nature lover so that such verses as I then achieved myself were almost bound to be about trees and fields and skies and seas. No bad thing if I had been familiar with the poets who knew how to deal with such material.' But his rural lyrics were based on what he had, since schooldays, read in Palgrave's *Golden Treasury*, 'on the weaker poems of Shelley and the more sugary ones of the Georgians':[12]

> The waters strive to wash away
>   The frail path of her melody,
> This little bird across the lake
>   That links her gentle soul with me.

Thomas's youthful affection for Tennyson is still in evidence:

> Like slender waterweeds to my mind
> The poplars wave in the great wind,

> And shoals of fishes are the leaves
> Which the smooth, rain-blurred air receives
> Within its silken stream.[13]

While these poems from the late 1930s remained unpublished, he found a sympathetic editor in Seamus O'Sullivan, who accepted several poems for publication in *The Dublin Magazine* in 1939–40: again these are for the most part lyrical evocations of the natural world and its delicacy:

> I know no clouds
> More beautiful than they
> That the far hills shroud
> At the end of the day.
>
> Silver and soft and grey
> As a wild bird's breast
> They cover the heath ways
> As a swan her nest,
>
> And as a lark sings
> To his mate from the deep sky,
> To these a shy star brings
> Peace from on high.[14]

At times the lyricism still shades into sentimentality ('shy star'). Clearly such rural lyricism was too delicate a medium by which to engage the robust actualities of the life in which Thomas now found himself at Manafon, the unromantic world of the hard struggle of the upland farmers against the weather, the landscape and the pressures of the market: 'Their life and their attitudes administered an inward shock to my Georgian sensibility. I responded with the first of my poems about Iago Prytherch, a sort of prototype of this kind of farmer. It was called "A Peasant".'[15]

What is remarkable is the rapidity of the shift in Thomas's poetic technique, from the gentle, not to say genteel, tones of the poems of 1939–40 to the flinty registers, often short-vowelled, hard-consonanted monosyllables, in which Iago Prytherch and his fellow hill workers are portrayed only three years later:

> Docking mangels, chipping the green skin
> From the yellow bones with a half-witted grin
> Of satisfaction, or churning the crude earth
> To a stiff sea of clods that glint in the wind –
> So are his days spent, his spittled mirth
> Rarer than the sun that cracks the cheeks
> Of the gaunt sky perhaps once in a week. (*SF* 14)[16]

We need to note, though, that changes in technique were already taking place in Thomas's poetry; the war, observed from Tallarn Green, had itself administered a shock to Thomas's perception of the world. M. Wynn Thomas has written perceptively of the ways in which a number of the lyric poems, written in this period and collected in *The Stones of the Field*, exhibit signs of 'a sensibility under stress'.[17] 'Propaganda' explicitly registers 'a chaos in the mind':

> Nor shot, nor shell, but the fused word,
> That rocks the world to its white root,
> Has wrought a chaos in the mind,
> And drained the love from the split heart;
>
> Nor shock, nor shower of the sharp blows,
> That fall alike from life and death,
> But some slow subsidence within,
> That sinks a grave for the sapped faith. (*SF* 10)

This is an altogether more discordant music, with the hard alliteration and those powerful monosyllables, and possibly a hint of Dylan Thomas in the last line. It is supposedly a poem about what propaganda does, the erosion of one's faith in truth; but the shot and shell are there too. As Wynn Thomas has suggested, the whole view of the natural world has, with this shock to the poet's imagination, started to shift; now the poetry registers not just larks and beautiful hills but also 'In the hushed meadows the weasel, / That would tear the soft down of the throat / and suck the veins dry / Of their glittering blood' ('On a Portrait of Joseph Hone by Augustus John', *SF* 35).

Thus one can argue that the 'more robust poetry' with which Thomas felt he needed to respond to the hill people of Manafon was already emerging under the pressures he experienced at Tallarn Green.[18] But the actual techniques he employed also drew on other sources. Patrick Crotty, for instance, has drawn attention to John Montague's detection of the 'releasing influence' of Patrick Kavanagh's *The Great Hunger* (1942) on 'other writers, from R. S. Thomas to Seamus Heaney', as well as Montague's less generous, and less accurate, later comment that Thomas 'was so impressed by *The Great Hunger* that he rewrote it twice in Anglo-Welsh terms', first as 'The Airy Tomb' and then as *The Minister*.[19] While finding the debt to Kavanagh in 'The Airy Tomb' to be merely 'suggestive rather than conclusive', Crotty's discussion indicates interesting points of connection between Kavanagh's poem and *The Minister* (1942), though Crotty also points to significant differences between the two poets and their work: Kavanagh develops no nationalist agenda in his portrayal of the Irish peasantry and, more fundamentally perhaps, while Thomas looks at the hill workers of Montgomeryshire overtly from the position of an outsider, Kavanagh was born and brought up in Inniskeen, County Monaghan, a son of rural Ireland, knowing its social pressures from the inside.[20]

But it seems clear that *The Great Hunger* was an enabling text, imaginatively and stylistically, for R. S. Thomas in more than just the two works Montague refers to (though this is not to say of course that Kavanagh was the only poet to contribute to the radical shift of style that takes place in Thomas's writing in the early 1940s, as we shall see). Moreover, while Thomas may have read Kavanagh's earlier work in the pages of *The Dublin Magazine* to which he was himself contributing, he would not even have had to purchase the Cuala Press edition of *The Great Hunger* when it was published in 1942, the very year Thomas arrived in Manafon: a portion of the poem appeared in the

January 1942 edition of *Horizon*, the journal which had published Thomas's 'Homo Sapiens' just months earlier.[21] The extract was entitled 'The Old Peasant' and the term 'peasant' is used at several points in the poem.

The title of Patrick Kavanagh's poem refers not, as one might first expect, to the desolating Irish famines of the mid-nineteenth century, but to a hunger which Kavanagh saw as continuing in the communities of rural Ireland: the starvation of the affections and the imagination, the thwarting of the possibility of emotional and sexual fulfilment, by the constraints of a parochial culture rooted in the teachings of the Roman Catholic church but above all by 'the grip of the irregular fields' from which 'No man escapes':[22] 'Life dried in the veins of these women and men' (*GH* 45). Kavanagh's protagonist, Maguire, works long, numbing, brutalizing hours alone in his fields, to support his sister and their mother, who lives on, nagging and chivvying, until Maguire himself is in his sixties and life – the possibility of a wife and children – has passed him by. Maguire's only outlet for his sexual starvation is lonely masturbation 'over the impotent cinders' late at night: he is married to his fields and in this community, anyway, 'Love' is 'The heifer waiting to be nosed by the old bull' (*GH* 47).

On his visits to the isolated hill farms of his own parish, Thomas found a similar hard existence, and lives that struggled with the same lonely unfulfilment; Kavanagh's poem gave Thomas access not only to ways of thinking about such lives, but also to ways of writing about them. In an uncollected poem,

> Gideon Pugh has a house of his own, but no wife
> To ease the loneliness of his wide bed,
> And the crickets, invisible under the cauldron
> Of simmering broth, are a poor exchange for children
> With their wearisome prattle on the bare hearth.
> He works all day, his thoughts trained to one furrow [. . .]

Night masks

> [. . .] his haggard face
> With its *starved* eyes brooding over the place.
> Leave him, then, leave him alone with his secret dream,
> The dream of a stone in the grass, the *hunger* of a tree
> For the soft touch of the sky, of the land for the sea.[23]

Kavanagh may have known the rural community from the inside, but the usual stance of the narrator, especially in the early sections of *The Great Hunger*, is overtly as guide to the uninformed reader, directing the reader's gaze, sharing the reader's questioning perspective:

> [. . .] the potato-gatherers like mechanised scarecrows move
> Along the side-fall of the hill – Maguire and his men.
> If we watch them an hour is there anything we can prove
> Of life as it is broken-backed over the Book
> Of Death?
>
> Watch him, watch him, that man on a hill whose spirit
> Is a wet sack flapping about the knees of time. (*GH* 34, 35)

It is a stance, the poet as guide to, and questioner of, the reader, as intermediary between reader and hill farmer that is characteristic of Thomas's Manafon poems, from the beginning:

> see him fixed in his chair   ('A Peasant', *SF* 14)
>
> See how the earth claims him as he passes by
>   ('The Mistress', *SF* 21)
>
> Shall we follow him down, witness his swift undoing
>   ('Out of the Hills', *SF* 7)
>
> A man is in the fields. Let us look with his eyes. ('Enigma', *AL* 31)
>
> Consider this man in the field beneath   ('Affinity', *SF* 20)

Kavanagh's poem might also have contributed to showing Thomas a way of freeing up his verse from the regular stanzaic patterns of his earlier Georgianism; *The Great Hunger* is for the most part written in free verse, with only the occasional couplet, and with considerable variation of line length between sections. While Thomas's first collection, *The Stones of the Field*, contains a number of rhymed poems, we also find him using a longer-lined free verse:

> Dreams clustering thick on his sallow skull,
> Dark as curls, he comes, ambling with his cattle
> From the starved pastures. He has shaken from off his shoulders
> The weight of the sky, and the lash of the wind's sharpness
> Is healing already under the medicinal sun. ('Out of the Hills')

At one point in the first section of his poem Kavanagh deploys a technique which to those coming to the poem from Thomas seems strikingly resonant of the Welsh poet:

> And the flints that lit a candle for him on a June altar
> Flameless. (*GH* 34)

The enjambement is echoed in 'A Peasant' ('see him fixed in his chair / Motionless'). This, though, is merely an early example of a technique which Thomas was to develop in his own ways and to deploy to great effect in his later poetry, where his use of line break can be deeply moving in its enactment of thought and feeling:

> I take their hands,
> Hard hands. There is no love
> For such, only a willed
> Gentleness. Negligible men
> From the village, from the small
> Holdings, they bring their grief
> Sullenly to my back door,
> And are speechless. ('They', *NHBF* 39)

Perhaps above all what Thomas would have found in *The Great Hunger* is a linguistic register appropriate to the way of life with which he was now confronted. In place of the romantic and often fanciful registers of Palgrave and the Georgians ('the bearded wind bends low and plays / The faint, frail songs of old', 'The Bridge'), Kavanagh presented a language which is direct, tactile, rooted in the world of the rural workers' daily toil – 'wet clay', 'weedy clods', 'mud-gloved fingers', 'The twisting sod' (GH 34, 35, 38) – a language unafraid to confront the unattractive physicalities of this life: 'deep in dung', 'grunts and spits / Through a clay wattled moustache', 'Coughed the prayer phlegm up from his throat and sighed: Amen' (GH 44, 35, 39). While Thomas's sensibility may initially have been shocked by 'the spittle and the phlegm of farm life', his imaginative response is strikingly immediate; as J. P. Ward points out, there is in the early poems written at Manafon 'a libidinous relish for immersion in the liquid, glutinous and messy', a relish frequently expressed in a register as tactile as anything in Kavanagh.[24] Indeed, Thomas's language, especially in its active verbs – 'wades', 'pull', 'suck', 'cling', dabble' – is, almost from the beginning of his work at Manafon, frequently even more energetic in its embrace of the messy physicality of farm life and the processes of the natural world. Presumably this 'relish' for that which will shock conventional tastes is a measure of Thomas's determination to emancipate himself from the bourgeois refinement of his upbringing; it is, in other words, another manifestation of his seeking for some new mode of life, a sense of wholeness that does not repress the physical, the 'unrespectable' levels of the self.

In this context, it is worth considering more closely the precise ways in which R. S. Thomas looks at Iago Prytherch and his fellow hill farmers and how that looking relates to our discussion of Thomas's uncertainty of identity and his related searching for a way of life where he can feel more fulfilled, where he can feel at home. In 'Which?' (T 42), Thomas asks 'And Prytherch – was he a real man . . .?' For, in fact, a sense of the unreal, of the uncanny, haunts a number of the poems in which Iago and the other hill workers are portrayed. Nicholas Royle has recently argued that

The uncanny involves feelings of uncertainty, in particular regarding
the reality of who one is and what is being experienced. Suddenly
one's sense of oneself [. . .] seems strangely questionable.[25]

We have already noted Thomas's susceptibility to such feelings, to
his seemingly uncertain grasp on identity – there was 'something
unreal' he says of his feelings of detachment from social activities
at Bangor. (Some of his accounts of childhood – 'To a sensitive
boy, ghosts were real enough' (*A* 30) – also incidentally suggest a
mind open to experiences of the uncanny in a more general
sense.) In terms of Freud's essay on which Royle is drawing,
such moments of alienation, of displacement, are manifestations
of the *unheimlich*, the 'unhomely', a profound sense of unease in
one's world, and one's identity, feelings which may be momentary
or more long-term. Royle in fact suggests that the uncanny may be
bound up with feelings of 'extreme nostalgia' or 'homesickness';
certainly we can relate Thomas's *hiraeth* for Anglesey, which he
in turn relates to his longings for the simple peasant life of the
Celtic west, to such states of feeling.[26]
    For Freud, while the uncanny 'is undoubtedly related to what
is frightening – to what arouses dread and horror', that dread
arises specifically from 'that class of the frightening which leads
back to what is known of old and long familiar';[27] in other words
what is disturbing about the *unheimlich* is its proximity to the
heimlich, that which is 'homely' or familiar. As Royle puts it, 'the
uncanny is not simply an experience of strangeness or alienation'
but can take the form of 'a peculiar commingling of the familiar
and unfamiliar'.[28] Approached in these terms, the confrontations
with Iago and the other labourers and farmers can clearly be
read in terms of the uncanny, and thus in terms of Thomas's own
insecurity of identity. In 'A Peasant' Iago is both strikingly
unfamiliar – the first fifteen lines of the poem insist on his
otherness from the world of civilized taste and values, the world
of the poet and the assumed reader – and then, the poet insists,
essentially connected *to* the reader: 'This is your prototype.' It is not
just 'the vacancy of his mind' that is 'frightening', but the very fact

that Iago, the reader and, implicitly, the poet are in fact not different but connected; one might indeed argue that what we have here is another aspect of the uncanny. For Freud argues that we can experience the uncanny when that which is usually hidden is brought to light, when something which we normally repress in ourselves is revealed.[29] Thomas's poem insists on just such a revelation.

The recognition of a fundamental connection between the humanity of the apparently uncouth hill workers and that of the reader recurs in these early poems, re-enacting one feels a recognition that Thomas has had to achieve, or perhaps more accurately, given the repetition of the idea, a recognition that he is still himself trying to come to terms with; the poems in other words are the sites of that struggle, with the 'you' recurrently encompassing both reader and the poet himself. 'Affinity' (*SF* 20) thus invites us to:

> Consider this man in the field beneath,
> Gaitered with mud [. . .]
> Without children, without wife,
> Stumbling insensitively from furrow to furrow,
> A vague somnambulist

and then asks

> From the standpoint of education or caste or creed
> Is there anything to show that your essential need
> Is less than his [. . .]
>   Don't be taken in
> By stinking garments or an aimless grin;
> He also is human, and the same small star,
> That lights you homeward, has inflamed his mind
> With the old hunger, born of his kind.

Within the unfamiliar is glimpsed something that is, disturbingly, the same. When the hill farmer speaks, albeit his 'life is smirched with dung', it is to insist 'Listen, listen, I am a man like you' (*AL* 17). The reader of 'The Labourer' (*AL* 32) is invited by the narrator to look at the man in the fields, his limbs 'wrinkled and gnarled', and to 'tell me what you think':

> A wild tree still, whose seasons are not yours,
> The slow heart beating to the hidden pulse
> Of the strong sap, the feet firm in the soil?
> No, no, a man like you, but blind with tears
> Of sweat to the bright star that draws you on.

While Freud, perhaps unsurprisingly, associates experiences of the uncanny with mist and fog, and Royle connects the uncanny with 'a strangeness of framing, [. . .] an experience of liminality',[30] in Thomas's poems repeatedly the figure on the hills or in the fields is seen in a half-light which adds to the sense of uncertainty, of insecurity of perception, which attaches to these poems. Repeatedly Iago or one of his fellow hill workers is seen at dawn or at evening, as the stars appear, or it is moonlight. Iago endures 'like a tree under the curious stars'; in the uncollected 'Welsh Shepherd', 'Poor Iago Prytherch' is 'wandering in the dew':

> At break of day behold him, alone with his few
> Hedge-shorn yearlings and his bitch at heel,
> A scarecrow of a man, becalmed in the unreal
> Tides of light.[31]

One notes again that 'unreal' light; J. P. Ward comments on the way in which in 'Soil' 'the scene is suffused with an eerie lunar light' and 'static, as in a dream';[32] 'eerie' – or uncanny. In 'The Gap in the Hedge' (*AL* 15) Prytherch is again seen in a liminal light:

> [. . .] framed in the gap
> Between two hazels with his sharp eyes
> Bright as thorns, watching the sunrise
> Filling the valley with its pale yellow
> Light, where the sheep and the lambs went haloed
> With grey mist lifting from the dew.

In this poem, indeed, Prytherch is more 'unreal', more spectral, than ever, a presence that haunts the poet's mind, more evidently 'there' in his consciousness than in the fields:

> Or was it a likeness that the twigs drew
> With bold pencilling upon that bare
> Piece of the sky? For he's still there
> At early morning, when the light is right
> And I look up suddenly at a bird's flight.

This sense of insecurity as to what is real and what is unreal, this uncanny sense of dislocation of the self, is present in another confrontation, described in what is one of the odder moments in Thomas's early writing. In 'The Depopulation of the Welsh Hill Country' Thomas refers to 'the poet who lives away out over the bog' whom he meets on the moor:

I was sitting one day in the dry grasses reading some verse when he came up. 'I often think,' he said by way of greeting, 'that there is more interest in the hills than anywhere else.' He looked around over the empty moors and drew in a deep breath. 'You can smell the sea today,' he exclaimed. He began to recite a poem he had written about the searchlights during a raid on Merseyside. I looked up at him with the wide, blue air around him, and a strange emotion came over me. He was haloed with the clear light and his face was alive, his eyes keen. (*SP* 21)

It is a curious, almost epiphanic moment; again we notice the effect of the light, not a half-light here but still somewhat unreal as it haloes the rural poet. But one also registers the subject of the poem he recites. Why, one wonders, is a poet who lives in the hills of Montgomeryshire, 'away out over the bog', writing a poem about a bombing raid on Merseyside? It is possible, of course, but it is altogether more likely to be a subject about which Thomas himself would write, having watched those bombers from Tallarn Green, less than three years previously. In other words, it is a poem in which one is uncannily uncertain as to which poet is which; the haloed rural poet becomes a curious mirror for Thomas, assuming indeed that the other poet actually exists at all, rather than being a creation of Thomas's concern that such figures of natural creative imagination *should* exist in the Welsh countryside. What one senses here, indeed, is an eerie moment of, again, insecure identity, manifesting itself in the phenomenon of the double, which Freud sees as one source of the uncanny, '[The uncanny] is marked by the fact that the subject identifies himself with someone else, so that he is in doubt as to which his self is, or substitutes the extraneous self for his own'.[33] Real or not, the rural poet seems to embody a state of being for which Thomas is seeking for himself: creatively alive and in assured possession of an identity that comes of feeling at home in his world:

> In his rough shirt-sleeves and his old cap he had all the beauty of a bog flower or a tree, or anything that had grown out of the grassy moor. And I realized that it was because he belonged there and was happy there. (*SP* 21)

Thomas's own search for a sense of belonging and secure identity, a search essentially enacted in his writing in the period, is inextricably tied up not only with his seeking to come to terms with the life of Manafon but with Wales itself, with the issue of how he could *be* a Welsh writer while not yet being able to write poetry in the language. Such matters were under active debate, as Thomas discovered, within the pages of Keidrych Rhys's *Wales*. *Wales* had originally been founded by Rhys as Wales's first attempt at an English-language magazine for new, even avant-garde writing; the first issue in the summer of 1937 had featured new work by Vernon Watkins, Glyn Jones and, on its front cover, a piece of visionary prose by Dylan Thomas. Publication of *Wales* had been suspended when Keidrych Rhys joined the army and when *Wales* began again in the summer of 1943 it had a very different agenda. In his Editorial Rhys announced:

> The policy of *Wales* [. . .] will be a serious and responsible one *towards* Wales. We are primarily a cultural magazine, cultural in the broadest sense. [. . .] The only propaganda it will recognise will be the truth.[34]

Rhys was clearly aware that his change in direction would not please everybody – 'The few specialist readers who might with reason have expected this number of *Wales* [. . .] to resemble the old magazine, which concentrated almost exclusively on new "experimental" writing, may betray some slight signs of disappointment in reading this statement' – but while there would still be some experimental writing, Rhys now had new priorities, born of his experiences in the intervening years:

[T]he war has made the Welsh realise that they are a nation with a country, a people, a culture and a tradition *different* from England's to fight for. There is a new wave of national feeling about among our people. There is, in truth, a Welsh renaissance.

Rhys's editorial points out to readers the recent publication of a parliamentary report on the future governance of Scotland – '*Wales* hopes to collaborate in pan-Celtic matters as much as possible in the future' – and now Wales 'must do more than talk about playing her part in the world. She must act.' This was rousing stuff, and the pages of this issue of *Wales* and those that followed contain a series of articles on Welsh culture and history, articles which address the issues of what it means to be Welsh and, repeatedly, what was the relation of 'Anglo-Welsh' writing to Wales and what contribution it could make to Wales's future. In 'A Note on "Anglo-Welsh"' Wyn Griffith dismisses the label as redundant, suspecting that it is merely 'an easy way of announcing to the English reader that the writer pre-judges the issue by claiming to be "different". If he is "different" his writings will show it.' On the next page, in his essay 'The Relevance of the Anglo-Welsh', W. Moelwyn Merchant is content to use the label, and is more concerned with what the role of the 'Anglo-Welsh' writer should be. Comparing those stories in Penguin's 1941 anthology *Welsh Short Stories* which have been translated from Welsh with those by Anglo-Welsh writers, Merchant sees the two groups of stories as having emerged from 'two almost wholly divergent cultures': the one springing from 'a community which still bears the marks of a tradition, a continuity of language and function in an agricultural environment', while the others 'show, in varying degrees, the break with this tradition and an attempt to come to terms with an alien mode of life – capitalist industrialism'. In Merchant's view, Wales's English-language writers have been too concerned with '*interpretation* – [with] explaining Wales to the English', a process which invariably results in simplification and caricature. In doing so these writers are leaving unfilled a much more important task, 'that of rendering self-conscious those elements in the Welsh social tradition which may profitably be perpetuated'. In other words 'interpretation in the first instance should serve the parent culture rather than the outside world'; the most valuable function for the 'Anglo-Welsh' writer 'is to re-integrate traditional values in the new social situation'.

The issue of the continuity of the Welsh tradition, its rootedness in the rhythms of the rural and the past, is a recurring theme in the debate in *Wales*. (Such a sense of continuity would have especial resonance, of course, in the insecurities of wartime.) This first issue of the revived *Wales* also contains a short but wide-ranging essay on 'The Welsh Poetic Tradition' by H. Idris Bell, in which he not only stresses that '*Continuity, tradition*, the sense of belonging to a sort of apostolic succession, of being a link in a chain, is central' to Welsh poetry, but he also emphasizes the social role of the Welsh bard – he was a 'public official' in the community, schooled in the traditions of his craft – a role quite foreign to the English: 'In his poetry, as in most other things, the Englishman is an individualist.' Thus for the Welsh, in either language, to borrow from this alien tradition is fraught with risk. While Bell asserts that 'it is in Welsh that the poetic genius of the nation has best expressed itself', he is of course aware of the context in which he is writing: 'If a Welshman loses his Welsh, he will still be recognizably a Welshman, and if he writes English poetry it is probable that a discerning eye will be able to discover in it Welsh characteristics.' Again, the 'Anglo-Welsh' writer in English must be distinctively Welsh, aware – the very presence of Bell's essay in *Wales* underlines the point – of the history, nature and techniques of Welsh-language poetry. (Glyn Jones ends his review, in the same issue, of Idris Davies's *The Angry Summer* by asking plaintively, 'Why does a Welsh poet writing in English so seldom reveal his acquaintance with Welsh?')

Continuity – of race, blood and tradition – is also the subject of a characteristically idiosyncratic essay in the same issue by John Cowper Powys entitled 'Welsh Aboriginals (or The Real Welsh)'. For Powys 'the real Welsh' are descended from the aboriginal people of 'Non-Aryan Berber blood' who inhabited Wales before the coming of the Celts. (Powys claims to be able to detect 'those among our Welsh writers who are the real thing and those whose tone and temper and attitude of mind betrays the Romanized Celt, or the Normanized Celt, or the Anglicized Celt, or an aggressive mixture of all three mixtures. [. . .] We *real Welsh* have for some little matter of ten thousand years inter-married solely and purely among ourselves.') Powys agrees with Iorwerth Peate's conviction that 'the inaccessibility of certain parts of our land [. . .] has saved our "remnant" of Real Welshmen', who are to be found in the fastnesses of the Welsh hill country. These true Welsh Powys sees as marked by, amongst other things, their deep sense of community and their 'incurable habit of regarding the system of things as a *Multiverse* rather than as a *Universe*', reluctant to accept the unified codes of the modern scientific and technological world: 'We are [. . .] simply amused by uniformities forced upon us from outside.'

Such debates on Welsh identity and on the nature and potential role of an English-language literature in Wales would, manifestly, have had deep personal resonance for R. S. Thomas as he read this issue of *Wales* at Manafon;[35] his response seems to have been immediate for the next issue contained five poems by R. S. Thomas, one, 'Frost', still showing signs of his earlier lyric style ('Waiting for the spring to come: / The green lispings, the gold shower') while 'The Labourer' and 'A Farmer' show him already engaging the life of the hill workers ('the age old war [. . .] / With the crude earth and the indifferent stone'). But 'Confessions of an Anglo-Welshman', a poem Thomas never collected, explicitly engages the issues being debated in *Wales*:

For my own country's part
Her lore and language
I should have by heart.
'Twas she who raised me,
Built me bone by bone
Out of the teeming earth, the dreaming stone.
Even at my christening it was she decreed
Uprooted I should bleed.
And yet for another's sake
No wound deletes,
No patriotism dulls
The true and the beautiful
Bequeathed to me by Blake ,
Shelley and Shakespeare and the ravished Keats.[36]

It is a slight but still revealing piece, especially if one assumes a measure of identity between the narrating 'Anglo-Welshman' and Thomas himself, showing the depth of the poet's sense of inner division ('Uprooted I should bleed') and again attributing that division to the nature of his education and upbringing; what is interesting here is the open acknowledgement of the continued pull of the English literary tradition in which he had been educated. (One notes that the 'uprooting' seems to be confirmed by his christening, the identification given by his parents; in 'Roles' it is again 'They' who 'named him'.)

But the essays in *Wales* provided Thomas with notions of Welsh identity to which he could feel personally responsive. His own essay in *Wales* on 'The Depopulation of the Welsh Hill Country' responds directly to the view of Iorwerth Peate, Cowper Powys and, in a subsequent essay, Rhys Davies ('These are the only Welsh; they will always exist, if left alone. They are of magic; leave them alone') that the rural folk of the Welsh hill country are the bearers of the identity and values of the Welsh past. Thomas's essay quotes the same rhyme which Powys quotes in his article to evoke the life of the Welsh uplands: '*I ninnau boed byw / Yn ymyl gwisg Duw, / Yn y grug, yn y grug*', and of course Thomas can warn from first-hand experience how perilous is the plight of this ancient tradition.[37]

Moreover, as Thomas sought to be taken inside the culture, to begin to belong to 'the true Wales' and to the Welsh poetic tradition, as enunciated by Bell, he found a notion of the poet not as an isolate, an individual expressing private feeling from society's margins, but as a figure with a role *within* the community, indeed with a responsibility to that community and the continuity of its values. Above all he found in the debates in *Wales* ideas with which to engage as he began to formulate his own idea as to what the role of the 'Anglo-Welsh' poet might be. In fact when asked in a feature in *Wales* in 1946 if he considers himself to be an Anglo-Welsh writer, Thomas answers firmly 'No! A Welsh writer' and, when asked for whom it is that he writes, he quotes Yeats: 'All day I'd looked in the face / What I had hoped 'twould be / To write for my own race / And the reality.'[38] In the same year in an essay on 'Some Contemporary Scottish Writing', he is dismissive of 'that foolish epithet, Anglo-Welsh' and in Hugh MacDiarmid he identifies a stimulating, uncompromising figure, like Saunders Lewis in Wales (whom Thomas had visited the previous year, to dedicate himself to Wales), a figure of literary authority who could lead his nation's cultural resistance to the influence of English colonialism, to 'the all-pervading twentieth century rationalism that goes hand in hand with western democracy and industrial development'; 'democracy' he here identifies with the bureaucracy of the modern mass society.[39] In the same essay Thomas sees signs that 'the mantle of writers like T. Gwynn Jones and W. J. Gruffydd is falling not upon the younger Welsh writers, but upon those of us who express ourselves in the English tongue', but their role as cultural leaders, 'winnowing and purifying [. . .] the people', should be to encourage 'an enlargement of national consciousness', perhaps 'a phase in the re-cymrification of Wales'. (Here, again, Thomas is echoing Keidrych Rhys, who in his editorial to the second issue of the revived *Wales* in 1943 had asked 'Is this Anglo-Welsh movement a stage on the way back to the use of Welsh for literature? I sincerely hope so.') Two years later, in an essay in *The Welsh Nationalist*, Thomas sets a clear agenda for 'Anglo-

Welsh' writers, quoting as he does so Moelwyn Merchant's 1943 essay in *Wales*; the writer must strive to reintegrate the life of the nation, heal the cleavage between the two traditions: 'if Wales is to live and retain its individuality, there must be continuity and awareness of that continuity'. Thus Anglo-Welsh writers must fulfil three tasks:

> Firstly, study, or as Wade-Evans would say, discover Welsh history. Secondly, steep yourself in the Welsh literary tradition. Thirdly, become acquainted with Welsh geology, geography, natural history and all other aspects of her life. And finally write out of that full knowledge and consciousness in English – if you can![40]

Thomas was evidently undertaking these tasks for himself: the poems collected in *The Stones of the Field* and *An Acre of Land* not only describe the life of the Montgomeryshire hills but allude to the *Mabinogion*, especially *Culhwch ac Olwen*, to Welsh folk-tales and to Welsh-language poetry.[41] Other poems refer to Welsh history: while in 'The Rising of Glyndŵr' (*SF* 17) the rebels are shadowy figures in the woods, 'The Tree' (*AL* 18–19), in which Glyndŵr speaks, is a more interesting poem as regards Thomas's nationalist thinking in this period. The lethargy of Glyndŵr and his people has been 'pierced' by the words of his poet, Gruffudd Llwyd. The brief period of Welsh independence, following Glyndŵr's defeat of the English, is characterized, again, in terms that emphasize the life of the Welsh as essentially communal; the life of this society is evoked by a first version of a scene which recurs through Thomas's writing as an evocation of the longed-for elusive life of emotional fulfilment, imaginative vitality and spiritual awareness:

> For one brief hour the summer came
> To the tree's branches and we heard
> In the green shade Rhiannon's birds
> Singing tirelessly as the streams
> That pluck glad tunes from the grey stones
> Of Powys of the broken hills.

The tree of the title is emblematic of Welsh independence; once more a life of fulfilment, of secure identity, is associated with being organically rooted in a particular place, a place where one can be at home. The image reappears in 'Welsh History', printed just a couple of pages after 'The Tree' in *An Acre of Land*, and this time Thomas's identification is explicit in the pronoun used throughout the poem:

> We were a people bred on legends [. . .]
> Clinging stubbornly to the proud tree
> Of blood and birth. [. . .]
>
> We were a people, and are so yet.

But as the poems explicitly point out, to make the tree flourish again will involve effort on their own behalf by the Welsh people, and perhaps sacrifice: 'he who sets his ear to the scarred bole, / Shall hear me tell from the deep tomb / How sorrow may bud the tree with tears, / But only his blood can make it bloom' ('The Tree'). For the pacifist, however, such notions of bloodshed are problematic. One notes, relatedly, how the final lines of 'Welsh History', first published as 'Welsh Nation', were changed from 'we will arise / And greet each other in a new dawn' in *An Acre of Land* to 'we will arise, / Armed, but not in the old way' in *Song at the Year's Turning*; possibly the original version was too suggestive in the post-war years of more negative connotations of nationalism.

It is evident too that Thomas was familiarizing himself with the techniques of the Welsh poetic tradition. In 1947, in what was almost certainly his first BBC radio broadcast, he notes that:

> a growing realization of the plight of my country, plus long pondering over the question of Anglo-Welsh writing, together with the desire to live up to the reputation for difference implied by the terms Welsh and Anglo-Welsh, have been responsible for certain experiments of mine both in subject matter and in technique. [. . .] For it seems to me that if we are unwilling to be called English poets, while at the same time we are averse from the title Anglo-Welsh, we have only the other to fall back on. But if we are to be known as Welsh poets then

our work must be a true expression of the life of our country in all its forms.[42]

He goes on to read 'Hill Farmer', pointing out that the poem contains 'a certain amount of internal rhyme and assonance' ('And he will go home from the fair / To dream of the grey mare with the broad belly, / And the bull and the prize tup / That held its head so proudly up') and points to the 'characteristically Welsh internal rhyme and alliteration' in 'The Hill Country, Montgomery-shire' (collected as 'The Welsh Hill Country', *AL* 7), which seeks to convey 'the tragedy of the decay of Welsh rural life'. Interestingly, Thomas has been looking not only back to the techniques of Welsh poetry but also, again, to the practice of contemporary Irish poets: 'The work of poets like Austin Clarke in Ireland has interested me, for he has shown how much of the atmosphere of old Irish verse can be brought into English by skilful counter-pointing.' In Clarke he found a writer who was seeking to express a modern Irish identity in his English-language poetic practice by establishing continuity with the Gaelic tradition in much the way that Thomas was trying to find continuity with the Welsh tradition.[43] His own experiment results in what he calls in the broadcast the 'strangely un-English sound' of a poem which he duly published in *The Dublin Magazine*, though one which he did not collect:

> Up in the high field's silence where
> The air is rarer, who dare break
> The seamless garment of the wind
> That wraps the bareness of his mind?
>
> The white sun spills about his feet
> A pool of darkness, sweet and cool,
> And mildly at its mournful brink
> The creatures of the wild are drinking.[44]

The rhyme of stressed with unstressed syllable here suggests a familiarity not just with Clarke but also with Welsh poetic practice. In 'Wales', with which Thomas ends the broadcast, he not only again uses 'consonantal counterpointing' but 'a good deal of falling assonance to suggest the tragedy of our position':

> Above the clatter of the broken water
> The song is caught in the bare boughs;
> The very air is veined with darkness – hearken!
> The brown owl wakens in the wood now. (*SYT* 47)

The use of half rhyme, internal rhyme and the rhyming of stressed and unstressed syllables recurs in the earlier work and even as he turns to free verse Thomas continues on occasion to create intricate aural effects (e.g. 'Here', 'A Line from St David's', 'So', 'Those Others').

At Manafon, however, far from finding a rural community living a way of life in which he could begin to put down roots and be at home, Thomas manifestly found himself set apart both by a way of life which was totally alien to him and by his very position as a priest. Not only had he to live amongst this community whose struggle was more with the things of this life, with wresting a living from the land, than with the things of the spirit, but he had to minister to them as their pastor; it would have been a challenge to any young priest – 'I found nothing that I'd been told or taught in theological college was of any help at all in these circumstances'[45] – but for a man with the idealistic longings which Thomas possessed at this time the challenge was all the more acute and deeply felt. The poems tell of a profound sense of incapacity in his role, of helplessness and, still, isolation: 'How do I serve so / This being they have shut out / Of their houses, their thoughts, their lives?' ('They', *NHBF* 39). In 'Evans' (*PS* 15) the narrator, presumably the visiting priest, is aware not only of the literal isolation of 'that sick man / I left stranded upon the vast / And lonely shore of his bleak bed' but of his spiritual isolation; while the image of 'the drip / Of rain like blood from the one tree / Weather tortured' recalls the message of Christ's salvation of man by His death on the cross, there is no hint that the priest has succeeded in conveying this message of hope. The poem expresses the narrator's sense of isolation as well as Evans's. While Thomas's poem for radio *The Minister* (1952) is manifestly not autobiographical – the protagonist is an unmarried Nonconformist minister under the thumb of his deacons, not an Anglican priest with a wife and child – the sense of isolation from his congregation which the Reverend Elias Morgan suffers would seem to owe something to Thomas's own experience.[46] At one point Thomas's narrator evokes a literally nightmarish experience:

> Did you dream, wanderer in the night,
> Of the ruined house with the one light
> Shining; and that you were the moth
> Drawn relentlessly out of the dark?
> The room was empty, but not for long.
> *You thought you knew them, but they always changed*
> *To something stranger, if you looked closely*
> *Into their faces.* And you wished you hadn't come. [. . .]
>   But when you got up to go
> There was a hand preventing you.
> And when you tried to cry out, the cry got stuck
> In your dry throat [. . .] (*SYT* 80, my italics)

This striking passage again evokes the dislocated mood of the uncanny ('a peculiar commingling of the familiar and unfamiliar'), of the *unheimlich*, which we have associated with insecurity of the self, an alienation of the self from one's surroundings, of not belonging.

Thomas speaks in his 1947 radio talk of 'my feeling for the earth and my preoccupation with the problem of the widening of the gap between man and the earth in the present era'. It was a feeling, as we have seen, born of personal need and, while he is aware of the socio-economic pressures on those who worked in the Welsh countryside, ultimately his constant reflection on the lives of the rural workers around him is born of the same need, his own profound inner questioning. These men *were* connected to the earth, and yet they often appeared not vital and imaginative

but passive, dull and unresponsive to the world around them
('blind / To it all', 'Enigma' *AL* 31), blunted by the unrelenting
routine of their work, not made authentic by the earth but
entrapped by it ('She dragged me down, / Slurring my gait first,
then my speech', 'The Slave', *SYT* 104). But at other times there is
an awareness of the comfort of the limited but secure life in
which shed blood 'seeps *home* / To the warm soil from which it
came' ('Soil' *AL* 28, my italics). In other moods Thomas sees his
flock almost as the inheritors of the imaginative life of the *hafod*:

> I have taxed your ignorance of rhyme and sonnet,
> Your want of deference to the painter's skill,
> But I know, as I listen, that your speech has in it
> The source of all poetry, clear as a rill
> Bubbling from your lips; and what brushworks could equal
> The artistry of your dwelling on the bare hill? (*SF* 29)

Such 'want of deference', the seemingly timeless, rooted resilience
of the hill folk – 'enduring like a tree' – represents a fundamental
challenge to Thomas's assumptions about the world, not just his
cultural values but his intellectual convictions. Ben Astley has
suggested that confronted by the 'anti-rational existence' of Iago
and his fellow hill farmers, 'Thomas is forced to re-evaluate his
own faith, not only religious faith but faith in his own understanding and in his ability to make sense out of the world', and, we
might add, his own place, his own identity, in it.[47] Astley shrewdly
sees the rejection of the inherited assumptions of Western metaphysics, based on the capacity of human reason to comprehend
the world, apparent in Thomas's later religious poetry, as having
its roots in his reflections at Manafon:

> Thomas seems to identify, in his meditations on Prytherch, a sense of
> spirituality alien to logical analysis. In the rare moments when
> Thomas achieves spiritual peace he usually identifies it with the
> letting-go of the mind's dominion.[48]

One such moment, as Astley points out, occurs in 'The Moor':

> There were no prayers said. But stillness
> Of the heart's passions – that was praise
> Enough: and the mind's cession
> Of its kingdom. I walked on
> Simple and poor, while the air crumbled
> And broke on me generously as bread. (*P* 24)

The stilling of the mind's activity represents a suspension, for the moment, of the ego, of the pressures of *self*-consciousness; it opens the possibility of communion with the world and with others, allows the possibility of love. The iconography of 'The Moor' is developed in 'Bread', where love is explicitly the transcendence of loneliness, the finding of community:

> Hunger was loneliness [. . .]

> He prayed for love, love that would share
> His rags' secret; rising he broke
> Like sun crumbling the gold air

> The live bread for the starved folk. (*PS* 46)

Chapter II
Eglwys-fach

In 1954, after twelve years at Manafon – and a few months before the poetic fruits of those years were to be published for the first time by a London publisher as *Song at the Year's Turning* – R. S. Thomas moved to the parish of Eglwys-fach, Cardiganshire, some twelve miles from Aberystwyth, where he became vicar of St Michael's. By now Thomas was a Welsh speaker and had published a number of essays and reviews in Welsh; he had been looking out for a vacancy in a Welsh-speaking parish, a place where he could come more fully inside the cultural community of Wales and realize himself more fully as a Welshman. Eglwys-fach seemed likely to fulfil his requirements: a rural parish in what appeared to be a Welsh-speaking area. However, if Manafon had been a shock to Thomas's values, Eglwys-fach turned out to be a profound, at times desolating, disappointment. There were Welsh-speakers in the parish, but it was English middle-class values, the very values he had been seeking to escape by the move back to Wales from Tallarn Green, that were in the ascendancy:

> What he didn't know before settling there was how weak the Welsh language was in Eglwys-fach. It was a parish of several large houses, and every one of them in the hands of the English, despite the Welsh names on almost all of them. The Welsh who did not farm were only gardeners and maids to these people. And even amongst the common folk of the village there had been quite a bit of intermarrying with English people from places such as Herefordshire. (*A* 64)

It was the English-language morning service for which the church was filled – the congregation and choir also included the boys from a local boarding school – while in the evening 'it was three or four of the faithful' who came to the Welsh Evensong. Moreover, the English people who occupied those large houses were 'retired tea planters, ex-army officers' (MS 12), people used to exerting authority in non-English cultures and to getting their own way. There were clear expectations of the role of the parish priest; Thomas's predecessor had been in the parish for twenty-five years, 'a safe conventional man, and therefore popular' (A 64). But relations between this dominant caste and a vicar who was a nationalist, a pacifist and a poet were always going to be difficult, and Thomas's lasting distaste for the military and colonial faction within the parish and the way they behaved is evident in his recollections of Eglwys-fach in *The Echoes Return Slow*: 'When the English colonise a parish, a vicar's is chaplain's work . . . officers' mess, receptions' (ERS 52). Such social occasions – never to Thomas's taste – are remembered graphically, in all their numbing falsity:

> 'How good of you to come!'
>   (Yawning inwardly.)
> So beautiful!
>   (The bitch!)
> Why cannot one avoid
> these sparrings?
>   [. . .] I move
> to a new partner, polishing
> my knuckles, dazzled by the medals
> he has left off. Once
> in the sand it had been his club
> against my fish-net. Here we exchange
> insults civilly. (ERS 53)

As well as the political and social values espoused by this element in the parish, it was the moral values, which as priest he had to confront, that also dismayed and alienated Thomas, the 'snobbery, jealousy and love of money' (A 65) and the way even these middle-class English parishioners were themselves divided into mutually antipathetic factions, factions between which he as vicar had to manoeuvre:

There are sins rural and sins social. Does a god discriminate? Education is the refinement of evil. The priest is required to make his way along glass-sown walls. It is easier to divide a parish than to unite it, except on Sundays. The smell of the farm-yard was replaced by the smell of the decayed conscience. (*ERS* 46)

Thomas had sought a place where he could feel more at home; in fact he found himself surrounded by what he saw as lives of inauthenticity and artifice:

> And this one with his starched lip,
> his medals, his meanness;
> his ability to live cheap off dear things.
>
> And his china-eyed children
> with their crêpe-de-Chine hair,
> product of a chill nursery,
>
> borrowing nastiness from
> each other, growing harder and thinner
> on the days' diet of yawns and smirks.
>
> His wife and his friends' wives,
> reputations congealing about their mouths[']
> cutlery after the prandial remarks. (*ERS* 47)

The depth of Thomas's animosity is evident even in these lines written some three decades later; inevitably his antipathy towards some in his flock found tart expression in the poetry he was writing at Eglwys-fach at the time:

> They stand about conversing
> In dark clumps, less beautiful than trees.
> What have they come here to mourn?
> There was a death, yes; but death's brother,
> Sin, is of more importance.
> Shabbily the teeth gleam,
> Sharpening themselves on reputations
> That were firm once. On the cheap coffin

> The earth falls more cleanly than tears.
> What are these red faces for?
> This incidence of pious catarrh
> At the grave's edge? ('Funeral', *BT* 10)

The bleak social satire is a new note in Thomas's work, the falsity of the mourners' grief measured against the authenticity of the natural world, the trees and the earth. The past tenses used in 'The Parish' might suggest a recollection of Manafon, but the attitude to the parishioners is unlike that which we find in the verse written there and is at least coloured by Thomas's experience at Eglwys-fach. (The reference to the 'main road' is also suggestive of the main road which cuts through the village of Eglwys-fach, past the church):

> There was part of the parish that few knew.
> They lived in houses on the main road
> To God, as they thought, managing primly
> The days' dirt, bottling talk
> Of birth and marriage in cold eyes;
> Nothing to tell in their spick rooms'
> Discipline how with its old violence
> Grass raged under the floor. ('The Parish', *T* 15)

Again, the concerns which fill the parishioners' busy lives are seen in all their petty artifice when placed alongside the authentic energy of nature; it is the farmer who feels its ambiguous power and who lives the fuller life: 'you had watched like me / The sharp tooth tearing its prey, / While a bird sang from a tall tree'.

It was above all the retired military officers who presented the greatest challenge: 'It is very difficult for an officer who has retired to convince himself that he has done so. And there is the vicar in front of him to remind him of his superior rank' (*A* 75). Here, of course, as a confirmed pacifist, Thomas's distaste would be at its sharpest, as is evident in the contempt-filled portrayal, quoted above, of the retired officer, with his 'starched lip, / his medals'. The poem probably recalls a man in the parish who was in fact a war hero, a major general who had been awarded the DSO three times; as Barbara Prys-Williams has pointed out, the sheer animosity in this poem is indicative of the way such men would touch a raw nerve in Thomas.[49] Not only did they represent militaristic values which he rejected, but they also perhaps represented at some level a reproach, a nagging anxiety that ultimately his stance during the war had had within it an element of fear, not just idealism; it is an anxiety that is very present in *Echoes*: 'When volunteers / were called for to play / death's part, stood modestly / in the wings' (*ERS* 21).

But ultimately of course Thomas had to minister to all elements and factions, whatever his personal feelings. In reflecting in his autobiography on his time at Eglwys-fach, Thomas meditates on the meaning of 'personality', on the often artificial social role the individual assumes: 'everyone there played some part' (*A* 74). The passage concerns the social pretensions of many in the parish, before moving on to reflect more generally on the role of 'personality' in society and the reasons for it: 'Can a man face life if he feels that he is no-one?' But the opening of the passage declares his underlying personal concern (Thomas of course writes about himself, as he does throughout *Neb*, in the third person): 'His hold on his identity had been weak from the start, but that had not mattered at Manafon, as there was so little need to show it amongst the common folk of that parish.' But at Eglwys-fach 'more pressure had been put on him to conform to the conventional type of parish priest. [. . .] And often, in order to keep the parish more or less united, the vicar would give in to some extent, except in matters of major principle' (*A* 74–5). But compromise for a man like R. S. Thomas came at a price, and the struggle to maintain a balance in his ministry between his own principles and the need to keep good relations in the parish ultimately resulted in profound inner divisions. The period is recalled in a poem of lacerating self-contempt:

A will of iron, perforated
by indecision. [. . .]

> Voyeur
> of truth because of an ability
> to lie sideways. One
> of life's conjurors, standing
> upside down on his conscience,
> producing out of a hat rabbits
> where his brains should have been. (*ERS* 59)

His poetry at the time was equally unrelenting, as the poet turns in on himself. 'Judgment Day', whether we take the poem to be occasioned simply by the poet scrutinizing himself in a mirror or by his imagining himself in God's presence after death and being shown an image of himself in life, is another piece of bleak self-scrutiny:

> Yes, that's how I was,
> I know that face,
> That bony figure
> Without grace
> Of flesh or limb;
> In health happy,
> Careless of the claim
> Of the world's sick
> Or the world's poor;
> In pain craven –
> Lord, breathe once more
> On that sad mirror,
> Let me be lost
> In mist for ever
> Rather than own
> Such bleak reflections. (*T* 20)

It is a stark self-portrait of a man confronting his own sense of bad faith, the sense of bleak directness being underscored by the movement between the short lines, accumulating self accusations, and by the stripped language. The poem is certainly, as John Ward has argued, 'confessional, not in the way of Lowell or Plath, but of Augustine in its more originary sense. To lay one's soul bare to God is both to own it and to own up to it';[50] the

poem ends with the poet praying to be allowed to '. . . go back /
On my two knees / Slowly to undo / The knot of life / that was
tied there'. Manifestly, the poem can be read as a judgement on
the way that the subject has responded to the 'knot' that his life
on earth as a whole has tied, but in context, one might speculate
that this painful poem arises out of the particular knot into
which Thomas felt himself being tied at Eglwys-fach. In this light
one might see the poem as being also related, once more, to a
renewed sense in Thomas of his weak hold on identity. The
image of the poet regarding himself in a mirror will recur
repeatedly in his later poetry, but it is perhaps appropriate to
register here the relation between such images and the uncanny.
In his essay on 'The Uncanny' Freud comments that:

> The idea of the 'double' does not necessarily disappear with the
> passing of primary narcissism [the self-regarding nature of the child],
> for it can receive fresh meaning from the later stages of the ego's
> development. A special agency is slowly formed there, which is able
> to stand over against the rest of the ego, which has the function of
> observing and criticizing the self and of exercising a censorship within
> the mind, and which we become aware of as our 'conscience'.[51]

We hardly need Freud to enable us to see that Thomas's poem
is about the operation of the conscience; however, when the
operation of the conscience becomes particularly acute and
stressful, that agency 'stand[ing] over the rest of the ego' becomes
a source of profound self-division and insecurity. In his essay,
however, as we have already noted, Freud sees one source of
feelings of the uncanny as being the individual's experience of a
double or an image of himself, where the 'subject identifies
himself with someone else, so that he is in doubt as to which
his self is'; Freud identifies a similar uncanny 'ego-disturbance'
as being experienced when 'meeting one's own image unbidden
and unexpected', as in a reflection or a mirror.[52] In other words,
'Judgment Day', as well as being a confessional poem, also
manifests a sense of anxiety about identity, a sense of the poet's
feeling 'not-at-home' in his life.

It is presumably not coincidental that it is in this period of intense inwardness and self-questioning that Thomas begins to write, albeit often in an oblique way, poems that take stock of his own life and the factors that have made him what he is. These poems – which have come to be examined by critics only relatively recently – consider the relations between his parents and the role he unwittingly played in that relationship: 'I was the bait / That became cargo, / Shortening his trips, / Waiting on the bone's wharf. / Her tongue ruled the tides' ('The Boy's Tale', *BT* 36, cf. 'Ap Huw's Testament', *PS* 29); his own tense relationship with his mother ('Mother and Son', *T* 37, where we note his plea to be allowed 'To find mirrors that do not reproach / My smooth face'); his relationship with his father ('The Fisherman' *NHBF* 19 and the moving 'Sailors' Hospital', *NHBF* 24–5 written after his father's death in 1965); with his wife: 'she loves me. I know how' ('Ap Huw's Testament'); and with his son ('Careers': 'Son, from the mirror / you hold to me I turn / to recriminate. That likeness / you are at work upon – it hurts', *NHBF* 7–8). One of the most poignant of these family/ autobiographical poems is 'Sorry' (*BT* 12): 'Dear parents, / I forgive you my life, / Begotten in a drab town, / The intention was good.' They have done their best for him, set him on the path – again the point is registered – to his present career:

> It was not your fault.
> What should have gone on,
> Arrow aimed from a tried bow
> At a tried target, has turned back,
> Wounding itself
> With questions you had not asked.

For them the career in the Church seemed a secure one, especially given their own social aspirations. But this was to assume a clerical life of conventional belief and acceptance of the social status quo; they could not know the nature of their son's mind, confronting questions they could not conceive, let alone ask: about belief, about the nature of his ministry but also about the very nature of his identity. In this period, indeed, as J. P. Ward has indicated, 'the poet experiences questioning as a normal state'.[53]

Above all he questions his role as a priest. Thomas could not ignore those in his parish at Eglwys-fach whose values were so different to his, and to the faith he and they professed, but the difficulty of his ministry is all too evident:

> We stand looking at
> Each other. I take the word 'prayer'
> And present it to them. I wait idly,
> Wondering what their lips will
> Make of it. But they hand back
> Such presents. I am left alone
> With no echoes to the amen
> I dreamed of. I am saved by music
> From the emptiness of this place
> Of despair. [. . .]
>   I call on God
> In the after silence, and my shadow
> Wrestles with him upon a wall
> Of plaster, that has all the nation's
> Hardness in it. They see me thrown
> Without movement of their oblique eyes. ('Service', P 36)

At Manafon he had struggled to bring the Christian message to a people who frequently could not comprehend – 'I whose invective would spurt like a flame of fire / To be quenched always in the coldness of your stare' – but there his congregation was relatively uneducated, and their priority economic survival. At Eglwys-fach it was different: here he faces a congregation that is middle-class, relatively financially secure, many of them well-educated. But there is no inclination to involve themselves emotionally and imaginatively in the things of the spirit; secure in what they believe ('A congregation at prayer / telling Him what he is like', ERS 55), they are content quietly to watch the priest perform, let him wrestle with his faith, while they remain detached, and unmoved. The 'despair' is his. In fact a number of poems in the period consider the life of the rural priest. In 'The Country Clergy'

(*PS* 28) Thomas reflects on the role of the clergy, seemingly in the past, 'working in old rectories [. . .] / Venerable men, their black cloth / A little dusty, a little green / With holy mildew'. Their quiet, unspectacular lives of study and parish work end with equally modest deaths: 'Toppled into the same grave / With oafs and yokels'. But they have had an impact on those to whom they have ministered; they have written 'On men's hearts and in the minds / Of young children sublime words' and while these words may be 'Too soon forgotten', the poem ends on a note of quiet faith: 'God in his time / Or out of time will correct this'. The firmness of the ending here comes as something of a surprise given the bleakness of poems like 'Service'. At the same time, perhaps, one senses the poet measuring his own ministry against the work of these unassuming men. The punningly titled 'Country Cures' (*BT* 8) also evokes the life of clergymen in 'Lost parishes, where the grass keeps / No register and life is bare / Of all but the cold fact of the wind'; these are not places like Eglwys-fach, with its main road, but they are places, the poet reflects to himself, 'where you might have been sent / To learn patience'. It is a quality which the poet seems to come to value, to hang onto, in this period: in 'There' (*P* 26) he considers again the bleak world of the farmer for whom life is 'an experiment / In patience' while, just a few pages later, in 'Aside' (*P* 29) Iago himself is remembered and urged to 'Turn aside' from the fast traffic of modern life: 'There is no forward and no back / In the fields, only the year's two / Solstices, and patience between'. But while those 'Lost parishes' in 'Country Cures' might be places where the soul learns patience, Thomas is again acutely aware of the fact that the very 'collars' of those men, the badges of their calling, also 'fasten them by the neck / To loneliness'.

If the experience of Eglwys-fach caused Thomas to reflect on his role of priest, the move from Manafon, which had provided such rich material in the early work, also seems to have resulted in something of a crisis in his life as a poet. The first volume of work written at Eglwys-fach, *Poetry for Supper* (1958), contains a number of poems about the process of writing, and the role of the poet. 'Composition' (*PS* 40) begins bleakly 'He never could decide what to write / About'; 'truth' is too painful: 'the pen's scalpel tip / Was too sharp; thinly the blood ran / From unseen wounds', while 'love' results only in a sombre beauty: 'slowly the blood congealed / Like dark flowers saddening a field'. On the opposite page in the collection, 'The Cure' (*PS* 41) begins with a question that is equally bleak: 'But what to do?' and portrays poets as vulnerable, depending on their own imaginative resources in the absence of commonly shared, authoritative values: 'Doctors in verse / Being scarce now, most poets / Are their own patients, compelled to treat / Themselves first'. But Thomas seems clear here about the social role of the poet, as teacher and healer of his/her culture:

> Consider, you,
> Whose rough hands manipulate
> The fine bones of a sick culture,
> What areas of that infirm body
> Depend solely on a poet's cure.

Poets reach areas of the social body that others – politicians, social planners, those who deal with the outer, material world – cannot reach: the imagination of the people, the spiritual values of the culture. In 'Death of a Poet' (*PS* 31), however, the poet has failed in his pastoral role; on his deathbed the poet can only force out one final word: 'sorry':

> Sorry for the lies, for the long failure
> In the poet's war; that he preferred
> The easier rhythms of the heart
> To the mind's scansion; that now he dies
> Intestate, having nothing to leave
> But a few songs, cold as stones
> In the thin hands that asked for bread.

Here explicitly, like the priest, the poet has been unable to fulfil his calling. The two old poets who, in a corner of an inn, debate the nature of poetic creativity in the volume's title poem, are totally ignored by their fellow drinkers: 'the talk ran / Noisily by them, glib with prose' ('Poetry for Supper', *PS* 34). 'To a Young Poet' (*BT* 11) gives another bleak, disillusioned vision of the poetic life: 'For the first twenty years you are still growing. [. . .] / It's the next ten / You cut your teeth on to emerge smirking / For your brash courtship of the muse'. But service of the 'cold queen' must continue – 'From forty on / You learn from the sharp cuts and jags / Of poems that have come to pieces / In your crude hands' – only to end, after a lifetime of struggle, in rejection:

> You are old now
> As years reckon, but in that slower
> World of the poet you are just coming
> To sad manhood, knowing the smile
> On her proud face is not for you.

In fact *The Bread of Truth*, from which this poem comes, contains some of the bleakest poems of the period, haunted by a sense of spiritual isolation. The loneliness registered in 'The Country Clergy' and 'Country Cures' is echoed by the poet's own ennui in 'Alone' (*BT* 34). 'The watcher at the window' looks out on a landscape that reflects his own dead mood:

> The wild duck came down once
> In the day; for the rest
> There were the blank hours to fill.
> [. . .] the leaves dropped
> Like slow rain from their boughs.

The poet seems driven deep within himself:

> Keeping my own
> Company now, I have forsaken
> All but this bare basement of bone,
> Where the one dry flame is awake. ('This', *BT* 42)

In this mood, repeated in 'A Country', all seems futile:

> At fifty he was still trying to deceive
> Himself. He went out at night ,
> Imagining the dark country
> Between the border and the coast
> Was still Wales [. . .] (*BT* 30)

He may go outside, but the careful enjambement at the end of the first line indicates where the real focus remains, and that darkness is manifestly not just a literal one. Again in 'Welsh Border' (*BT* 9) 'it is a dark night', a phrase the resonance of which Thomas would have been all too aware; the poem ends 'The real fight goes on / In the mind; protect me, / Spirits, from myself'. The poet seems fearful of quite how far into the dark he might go in his isolation. Even God seems notably absent in these poems; the invocation to the rather enigmatic 'Spirits' seems to be to the spirits which haunt these dark borderlands, in that that they represent anything outside himself at all. Thomas's portrayal of Wallace Stevens, also in *The Bread of Truth*, constructs a figure who inhabits a similarly dark world:

> Words he shed
> Were dry leaves of a dry mind,
> Crackling as the wind blew
> From mortuaries of the cold heart. [. . .]
> He limped on, taking despair
> As a new antidote for love. (*BT* 25)

We notice that 'dry' echoing the 'dry flame' in 'This' (*BT* 42). For Thomas tellingly ignores the ludic, sensually rich, exotic side of Stevens entirely; the portrait of Stevens he creates is painted in the colours of Thomas's own dark mood.[54]

At times there seems to be an impatience with his own passivity, feeling that he is, as in his youth, being acted upon rather than feeling in control of his own life. In 'Who?' (*P* 39) he asks 'Someone must have thought of putting me here; / It wasn't myself did it', echoing the words of Mark Puw in the grim 'Gospel Truth', which appears in the same collection (*P* 32–4):

'Who put me here?' But there is no direct sign of a transcendent creator in either poem. In 'Who?' the poet seems detached from the world around him; he records its loveliness, but does so in tones which register more his sense of its sheer monotony and the ultimately illusory nature of such beauty:

> Annually the grass comes up green;
> The earth keeps its rotary motion.
> There is loveliness growing, where might have been truth's
> Bitterer berries.

Again the enjambement, particularly after the long line, gives the negative adjective increased impact. In the second stanza, it becomes evident in fact that the poem's title refers not so much to the question of the identity of who 'thought of putting me here' but, once more, to the identity of the speaker himself:

> But there's an underlying despair
> Of what should be most certain in my life:
> This hard image that is reflected
> In mirrors and in the eyes of my friends.
> It is for this that the air comes in thin
> At the nostril, and dries to a crust.

For the priest, 'What should be most certain in my life' is his faith in the order of things, in God's creation, and himself as part of it. But here for the speaker, alienated from the world around him, there is no certainty as to 'who' he is. He sees himself this time not in one mirror but in a nightmarish plurality of mirrors; he sees multiple reflections of his 'image'. But what he is at the same time despairingly aware of is the discrepancy between this social image (with presumably a pun on 'hard', that is, both a clear image and the hard external image that he has constructed) and his true self. Again, in other words, we sense that weak 'hold on his identity' (A 74), presumably born of a sense of the role-playing he is forced into as vicar at Eglwys-fach. Such a reading throws light on the significance of the graphic but somewhat enigmatic 'This To Do' in the same collection:

> I have this that I must do
> One day: overdraw on my balance
> Of air, and breaking the surface
> Of water go down into the green
> Darkness to search for the door
> To myself in dumbness and blindness
> And uproar of scared blood
> At the eardrums. [. . .]
>   I must go down with the poor
> Purse of my body and buy courage,
> Paying for it with the coins of my breath. (*P* 12)

Christopher Morgan's comments on the poem in his recent study are much to our purpose:

> Underpinning the poem as a whole is an experience of dislocation or alienation in which a 'surface' self is clearly conscious of an alternate hidden or 'buried self', the recovery of which is fraught with difficulty and danger. [. . .] The search is essentially hopeful and aimed at a reunification of the divided self.[55]

At the same time, though, the poem seems ultimately to be more aspirational than unambiguously hopeful. As Morgan himself notes, that phrase 'One day' suggests something of a 'recoil from the bold approach of the opening line'; what one is mainly conscious of is the poet's awareness of the effort that will be required, rendered in the poem in vivid physiological terms.

Revealingly, when Thomas looks back to his time at Eglwys-fach in *The Echoes Return Slow* he writes of a profound fear of extinction of self:

> An obsession with nothing
> distinguished him from his co-
> thinkers. From dreaming about
> it, he woke up to its immense

presence, to a consciousness
of when he was not, to
the equal certainty
of his being extinguished. (*ERS* 49)

The nightmarish vision again suggests something of the uncanny; certainly there is present a feeling of exclusion from any sense of wholeness, and at-homeness: 'There was a hope / he was outside of, with no-one / to ask him in' (*ERS* 49). One poem of the period, very different in tone from the bleak poems we have been considering, at the same time perhaps throws some light on them. In 'Abersoch' (*T* 21) – interestingly it appears in *Tares* on the page facing the anguished 'Judgment Day' – while the air is 'full of thunder and the far air / Brittle with lightning', what the poet recalls is the ordinary, tranquil scene in the foreground:

> [. . .] that girl
> Riding her cycle, hair at half-mast,
> And the men smoking, the dinghies at rest
> On the calm tide.

When the poet reflects on why it is that he remembers 'these few things' that seem in retrospect to be mere 'rumours of life, not life itself / That was being lived fiercely, where the storm raged', he wonders

> Was it just that the girl smiled,
> Though not at me, and the men smoking
> Had the look of those who have come safely home?

It is rather a striking explanation. For the poet, real life, 'life itself', is anything but tranquil, is inseparable from tumult and stress, and yet what his memory has clung to are these images of calm, which he associates, revealingly, with having come home. Equally revealing, and in context movingly, this is something that happens to 'those', not to himself.

Perhaps inevitably given the pressures he felt at Eglwys-fach, Thomas looked back to Manafon, where the realities of life, however hard to deal with, were clear and where he had ultimately begun to establish his personal and poetic bearings. The retrospective attractions of the familiar are registered early in the first collection Thomas published after the move to Eglwys-fach:

> The temptation is to go back,
> To make tryst with the pale ghost
> Of an earlier self, to summon
> To the mind's hearth, as I would now,
> You, Prytherch, there to renew
> The lost poetry of our talk
> Over the embers of that world
> We built together [. . .] ('Temptation of a Poet', *PS* 14)

Immediately the poet sees his situation as alienated from a previous identity, remembered now as settled and inextricably bound up with the company of Prytherch. The present is seen once more in terms of division, the expression unusually direct and plaintive:

> Prytherch, I am undone;
> The past calls with the cool smell
> Of autumn leaves, but the mind draws
> Me onward blind with the word's dust,
> Seeking a spring that my heart fumbles.

The 'mind' that draws Thomas on may at one level be his sense of duty to engage the new responsibilities that face him, but the poem's title suggests that the primary meaning is that the poet feels that his poetry must move on, should engage his new environment. However, that reference 'to the world's dust' is a telling one; consistently in Thomas's work 'dust' is associated with those things to which he feels most antipathetic – materialism, the grinding wheels of industrialism, the arid, and to Thomas inauthentic, life of the urban world. Thus, for example, the protagonist in

'Rhodri' (*P* 7) has left his 'homeland' to make his fortune in an English town: 'He moves in a landscape of dust / That is sourer than the smell / Of breweries'; other expatriates lose 'The cold stream's sibilants' and find their tongues 'coated with / A dustier speech' ('Expatriates', *PS* 42); in 'Arrival', however, the almost visionary village in the Welsh hills, where 'A bird chimes / from a green tree' near a river, is 'dust free' (*LP* 203).

In fact, in the volumes of the 1960s the poet repeatedly yields to the 'temptation' to look back to the life of Iago and the men of the Montgomeryshire hills. But now they are no longer seen as disturbingly 'other' but remembered with some nostalgia. Their rootedness, their patience and resilience, the authenticity of their struggle, is evoked in turn as measure of and rebuke to his own sense of insecurity, division and inauthenticity. In 'Absolution' (*PS* 44) the poet again looks back from 'the world's roads', where 'I have worn my soul bare' to address Iago directly:

> Prytherch, man, can you forgive
> From your stone altar on which the light's
> Bread is broken at dusk and dawn
> One who strafed you with thin scorn
> From the cheap gallery of his mind?

Again Iago is perceived – or rather recreated – in tones of half-light, but his possession of such calm authority is new. As he stands at his 'stone altar', we have the paradox of the poet-priest (albeit we are importing the latter role from outside the poem) seeking forgiveness from this 'ordinary man'; Iago is associated with the imagery of the broken bread, with communion and fellowship, a potent image for the implicitly lonely speaker. At the same time, despite this sense of assurance, and the lovely tranquillity that is evoked – '[I] come now with the first stars / Big on my lids westward' – the poet does not allow what he knows of the uncommunicative actuality of Iago to soften into sentimentality: the poet sees 'with the slow lifting up of your hand / No welcome, only forgiveness'.

In other poems, too, Thomas now reconsiders and directly reflects on the way he had looked at the hill farmers and the exact nature of what they meant – and mean – to him: 'Did I look long enough or too long?' ('The Face', *T* 17), 'And Prytherch – was he a real man, / Rolling his pain day after day / Up life's hill? [. . .] / Or was a wish to have him so / Responsible for his frayed shape?' ('Which?', *T* 42). But there is no doubt in the poet's mind as to the impact the hill farmers have had on him, on his emotional resources. In 'He' (*BT* 46), Iago is not only remembered with unusually direct affection ('Dear!'), but is seen as the inculcator of human understanding and love:

> He has become part of me,
> Aching in me like a bone
> Often bruised. Through him I learn
> Emptiness of the bare mind
> Without knowledge, and the frost
> Of knowledge, where there is no love.

Perhaps aware of the ways his capacity for such feelings is being tested at Eglwys-fach, the poet looks back again in 'The Dark Well' (*T* 9) to Prytherch as 'the man / Who more than all directed my slow / Charity where there was need' (punningly indicating both that his charity was directed to where it was needed, and also that he *needed* to have his charity directed/encouraged). We notice, too, the way the pronouns in this poem record the shift that has taken place in the relationship between poet and Prytherch: whereas in the earlier poetry the narrating poet invited the reader, 'you', to look/regard/consider the enigmatic hill farmer, from whom both poet and reader were distanced, Prytherch and the poet are now joined in an implicit 'us', as opposed to the 'They' who 'see you as they see you, / A poor farmer with no name'. However, if Iago's emotional resources are deeper than those of the poet – his 'heart, fuller than mine / Of gulped tears', again a measure of the emotional aridity we have noted the poet as experiencing – his well of feeling has been filled by the painful struggle of his life. These poems of the Welsh hills, written from Egwlys-fach, do not lose sight of the social and economic realities which, Thomas is all too aware, the folk of the hills face, the pressures that are slowly and inexorably forcing them from their farms ('Eviction', 'Afforestation', 'Encounter', 'Movement'); there is a recurrent undertone of grief. But the emblematic Iago, the figure that the poet sees 'When I close my eyes', remains unchanged: 'He will go on; that much is certain'; whatever is actually happening on the Welsh hills, 'on the walls / Of the mind's gallery that face / With the hills framing it will hang / Unglorified, but stern like the soil' ('The Face', P 41–2). We notice 'that much is certain': in the sometimes anguished insecurities of Eglwys-fach, the memory of Iago Prytherch provided invaluable inner resource.

There is a particular irony in the sense of stress and inner division that R. S. Thomas seems to have experienced at Eglwys-fach. Not long before leaving Manafon he had written to Islwyn Ffowc Elis:

> As you know by now my medium would be Welsh had I been correctly brought up, but I have to write in a foreign language because my grasp of it is better. But I shall not be satisfied with this situation while I live. This is the damage history has wrought on one such as myself – it has split my personality.[56]

Thomas had continued to learn Welsh with a local non-conformist minister, H. D. Owen, and the move to what he assumed was 'a Welsh-speaking parish', where he would 'not always have to travel outside the parish to use the Welsh language' (A 62), was an attempt to alleviate this fundamental sense of inner conflict; he may not be able to write poetry in Welsh but at least he would be able to live more of his life in the language. This would be the next stage in the process, begun at Tallarn Green, of remaking himself as wholly Welsh (in his own cultural terms), to live within a culture whose sense of rootedness and authenticity he could feel a part of, and at last be at home. The terms Thomas uses in an uncollected review he wrote in *The Listener* in 1958 of some guides for travellers in Wales are in this context revealing:

> But without the key of the Welsh language one and all must needs pass by the door that opens on the real Wales. [. . . The Welsh] are a homely people; they live in their kitchens. They have their front parlour, of course, and without the language the traveller will never get beyond it, however comfortable or uncomfortable he may feel. Nor is this to say that the kitchen is always the best place. But it is there that the Welsh are at home.[57]

But Eglwys-fach, as we have seen, was far from being a Welsh community in which he could feel at home. Moreover not only was the language weak, the houses with Welsh names occupied by members of the English middle classes whom Thomas saw as having 'colonise[d]' (*ERS* 52) the parish, but the local Welsh people seemed perfectly content with the situation. When the church filled for the English service on a Sunday morning, 'The Welsh would also be there to experience some of the glory!' (*A* 64); when Thomas himself pressed the local Welsh speakers to make more use of their language, he was regarded as 'a bit of a Welsh fanatic'.[58]

This thwarting of his personal expectation not only fuelled his antipathy towards many in the parish, from the outset, but also added to his growing disillusionment with the wider situation in Wales ('[. . .] most of our fellow-Welshmen are not worth bothering about', he had written to Islwyn Ffowc Elis in the letter quoted above) and deepened his own sense of alone-ness. It is this mood which colours the opening poem in the first of his Egwys-fach collections, 'Border Blues', a poem which, symptomatically, utilizes the fragmented, multi-voiced technique of Eliot's *The Waste Land*. As in Eliot's poem, echoes from the past, from a time when cultural values were coherent and personal identity secure, resound in the consciousness of the protagonist, as he wanders alone through a world in which coherence and continuity have been replaced by fragmentation, spirituality by materialism and triviality. The fragments from the richness of the Welsh past which Thomas's protagonist hears, or remembers – the words of St Beuno, a line from *Canu Heledd*, mourning Welsh defeat in battle, a snatch of an eighteenth-century ballad (*Mi sydd fachgen, ifanc, ffôl*) – are abruptly, and poignantly, juxtaposed with a Welsh present of cars and machinery, dance halls, pop songs and bus trips to the pantomime in Shrewsbury ('It was "The Babes" this year').[59] At times in the poem, the depth of Thomas's distaste causes national concerns to be cut across with class animus – 'Beuno had vanished, and in his place / There stood the ladies from the council houses: / Blue eyes and Birmingham, yellow / Hair, and the ritual murder of vowels' – in tones that Dafydd Elis Thomas has suggested recall the contempt of Saunders Lewis in 'Difiau Dyrchafael' ('Ascension Thursday'): 'O men, come forth / From your council houses'.[60] But the sense of alienation in the poem is powerfully realized:

> Excuse me, I said, I have an appointment
> On the high moors; it's the first of May
> And I must go the way of my fathers
> Despite the loneli – you might say rudeness. (*PS* 10)

Even as the poet evokes the idealized life of the Welsh folk in the high pastures which Thomas had constructed from his reading of Macleod and Yeats, the communal vision is undermined. The 'loneliness' he starts to express is made poignantly vivid by the empty actuality of the high moor:

> What am I doing up here alone
> But paying homage to a bleak, stone
> Monument to an evicted people?

The sense of displacement and rootlessness which Eliot's protagonist experiences is repeatedly dramatized in *The Waste Land* in episodes of what we can, clearly, identify as the *unheimlich*: uncanny, nightmarish moments of uncertainty as to the reality of the world around him and of his relation to it, from the experience of the 'Unreal City' in the first section to the eeriness of 'What the Thunder said'. While Thomas's poem does not have the same sustained sense of neurosis, his un-homed protagonist also experiences disturbing moments of the uncanny and hallucinatory:

> But Arthur leers
> And turns again to the cramped kitchen
> Where the old mother sits with her sons and daughters
> At the round table.

(It is a curious and personally revealing vision: the masculine Celtic hero reduced, once more, to domesticity.) The theme of the displacement of the Welsh from their homeland is engaged again in 'Eviction', and again it is evoked in terms of the narrator's first-person experience of the uncanny; what seems familiar becoming disturbingly other:

> Sometimes I lean on a patched gate,
> Thinking I see you at the grass
> With your long scythe: sometimes I hail you
> In your own tongue, and as in a dream
> A dear face coming up close
> Spits at us, the reply falls
> In that cold language that is the frost
> On all our nation. No it is not you,
> But someone who has taken your name,
> Your work, your home. (*BT* 13)

Thus even as Thomas finds there is essentially no Welsh community in Eglwys-fach which he could enter and feel at home in, he looks to engage himself in the wider condition of Wales. (It is presumably not entirely coincidental that he says of the figure in 'A Lecturer' [*BT* 31], usually taken to be the poet Gwenallt, that he will 'take you / Any time on a tour / Of the Welsh language', that 'his quick smile / Of recognition' is 'a cure / For loneliness'.) Though Thomas had attended a demonstration in 1951 organized by Plaid Cymru against the extension of an army camp at

Trawsfynydd, Islwyn Ffowc Elis suggests that he had had to persuade Thomas to attend and that he had little enthusiasm for the Party – *'Dydi'r Blaid yn gwneud dim byd'* ('Plaid aren't doing anything').[61] But by the mid-1960s the nationalist movement had found new energy: inspired by Saunders Lewis's radio lecture *Tynged yr Iaith* (The Fate of the Language) in 1962, forecasting the death of the Welsh language if the Welsh did not take action to save it, *Cymdeithas yr Iaith Gymraeg* (The Welsh Language Society), founded the same year, had embarked on a campaign of non-violent, direct action to gain new status for the language. Plaid Cymru itself found new confidence after the election of its leader, Gwynfor Evans, as its first MP in the Carmarthen by-election of 1966, followed by strong performances by the party in by-elections in Labour strongholds in the south Wales valleys. Thomas had addressed the situation in Wales in poems written while at Manafon, poems which tended to look back to the Welsh past and, implicitly or explicitly, compared the energies of more heroic times with the inertia of the present. Wales was at times seen in sombre, melancholic, even elegiac tones: 'There is no present in Wales, / And no future / There is only the past' ('Welsh Landscape', *AL* 26). But in the 1960s, aware of this new energy abroad in Wales, Thomas addressed the contemporary situation with new directness and in tones not of sadness but of anger and bitterness, fuelled one assumes by what he had experienced at Eglwys-fach. The final poem in *The Bread of Truth*, 'Looking at Sheep', in fact expresses this new engagement directly:

> Seeing how Wales fares
> Now, I will attend rather
> To things as they are: to green grass
> That is not ours; to visitors
> Buying us up. Thousands of mouths
> Are emptying their waste speech
> About us, and an Elsan culture
> Threatens us. (*BT* 48)

The tone and the graphic imagery – Elsan is a chemical product that breaks down human waste in the toilets used by campers and caravaners: the English language and its way of life are thus associated with excrement – is not unusual in Thomas's poems about Wales in the 1960s. Indeed the scatological images recur: 'Where can I go, then, from the smell / Of decay, from the putrefying of a dead / Nation?' the poet asks in 'Reservoirs' (*NHBF* 26); in 'Resort' (*NHBF* 23) the visitors from the towns who troop, dull-eyed and zombie-like, to look at the sea will ultimately 'return to the vomit / Of the factories' (as dogs return to their vomit). Such extreme registers, while manifestly expressing the intensity of the poet's anger and desperation, can at times thin the imaginative and emotional texture of a poem; this certainly happens in some of Thomas's slightly later poems on Wales: in 'Toast' (*WA* 37), for instance, maggots burrow in the carcass that was once Wales and:

> The stench, travelling on the wind
> out of the west, was the lure for more
> flies, befouling our winding-sheet
> with their droppings

while in 'A Land' (*WA* 43) the inhabitants:

> have hard hands that money adheres
>   to like the scales
> of some hideous disease, so that they grizzle
> as it is picked off.

While it can be argued that such poems have a bleak satiric power, such strident, lurid images ultimately tend to unbalance the poems, to tip them, to use Yeats's distinction, closer to mere rhetoric than to poetry.

Nor is Thomas's vituperation reserved for the English tourists and capitalists; some of his fiercest invective is aimed, as in this latter poem, at the Welsh themselves, for the way their materialism has overcome their self-respect, for the way they have, as a result, willingly acceded to the erosion of their native culture. While in 'Reservoirs' the Welsh language is being elbowed 'Into the grave that *we* have dug for it' (my italics), in 'Traeth Maelgwn' (*NHBF* 20) 'The few casual cowries / With which we are fobbed off' are gratefully accepted by the Welsh, like simple natives accepting the (ultimately worthless) largesse of the colonizing culture. While the late 1960s saw the surge in support for Plaid Cymru, the demonstrations by Cymdeithas yr Iaith, as well as the sporadic but violent activities of the Free Wales Army, these years also saw, presumably not coincidentally, preparations begin for the investiture of Prince Charles as Prince of Wales at Caernarfon in 1969: thus nationalist feelings could be diverted into more acceptable channels, allowing the Welsh to express their sense of national identity but to do so within the context of loyalty to the British Crown. Thomas's response (in 'Loyalties', *NHBF* 31) was predictably sardonic. While a large proportion of the Welsh public might express their loyalty – 'The prince walks upon the carpet / Our hearts have unrolled / For him' – accompanied by the usual marketing of Wales ('The shopkeepers are all attention'), Thomas grieves for what has been lost from Wales: the public celebrations in Caernarfon are in every sense far from the reality:

> Of the holding where Puw lived
> Once, wrapping the language
> About him, watching the trickle
> Of his children down the hill's side.

When the poet ventures to the capital of the British State in 'A Welshman at St James' Park' (*P* 23), he finds himself

> [. . .] invited to enter these gardens
> As one of the public, and to conduct myself
> In accordance with the regulations;
> To keep off the grass and sample flowers
> Without touching them

and his thoughts turn from such a formalized version of nature to the freedom of a Welsh hill

> That is without fencing, and the men,
> Bosworth blind, who left the heather
> And the high pastures of the heart.

The poet, clutching his return ticket, will travel in the opposite direction but, as M. Wynn Thomas has pointed out, in returning at the end of the poem to 'the high pastures of the heart', Thomas 'heads implicitly back not to a particular Welsh community. [. . .] he simply exchanges a state of exile for a state of internal exile'.[62] For if most of his fellow Welshmen remain 'Bosworth blind', willing to orientate themselves by the values of commerce and consumerism, then Thomas can only *remain* an outsider, even in Wales. In his discussion of this poem, Wynn Thomas relates the poet's blunt refusal to be 'one / Of the public' to Kierkegaard's view, in *The Present Age*, of 'the public', of mass society, as a constraint on the capacity of the individual to live authentically, according to his/her personal ideal of what life should be: 'no single person who belongs to the public makes a real commitment'.[63] This sense of the possible *necessity* for apartness has particular poignancy for a man like Thomas whose whole imaginative need, as we have seen, has been to find a home community, a 'true Wales' where he can feel fulfilled as an individual. Such images of a *necessary* apartness recur in Thomas's poetry in the 1960s. In 'The Untamed', for example, again a garden, albeit this time a private one, is juxtaposed to the freedom of the natural world:

> The old softness of lawns
> Persuading the slow foot
> Leads to defection; the silence
> Holds with its gloved hand
> The wild hawk of the mind.
>
> But not for long, windows,
> Opening in the trees

> Call the mind back
> To its true eyrie; I stoop
> Here only in play. (*BT* 33)

One notes the strength of 'defection'. The temptation in this garden, it would seem, is to a surrender of self, of a lapse into 'softness' and the domesticated; at the end, once again, the escape is back to the elemental world, as an image of the individual's lonely struggle for authenticity. Again, one catches an echo of Kierkegaard:

> Carking care is my feudal castle. It is built like an eagle's nest upon the peak of a mountain lost in the clouds. No one can take it by storm. From this abode I dart down into the world of reality to seize my prey; but I do not remain down there, I bear my quarry aloft to my stronghold. My booty is a picture I weave into the tapestries of my palace.[64]

The price of such integrity, it would seem, is aloneness, a sense of being without a home in the world. In his piece on 'The Welsh Parlour' in *The Listener* in 1958, Thomas had commented that the Welsh 'are a *homely* people; they live in their kitchens. They have their front parlour, of course, and without the language the traveller will never get beyond it'.[65] But when he addresses similar themes in 'Welcome' (*BT* 24) – the visitor 'must stop at [. . .] / The old bar of speech' – the image he uses for the Welsh language, as Wynn Thomas notes, is no longer one associated with the warm kitchen hearth of the homely Welsh:[66]

> Past town and factory
> You must travel back
> To the cold bud of water
> In the hard rock.

Even as the image picks up the association of language with the pure streams of the Welsh hill pastures, an association which recurs in the poems about the hill farmers, its main connotations now are of rigour and purity, resilience and resistance. Such qualities are embodied in the poems of the 1960s and in the later poems collected in *Welsh Airs* (1987) not in terms of communality but in images of exceptional individuals, usually isolated from or marginalized by their community, individuals who remain true to their own unique vision. The eye of Dic Aberdaron, the eccentric autodidact, reveals a

> light
>
> generated by a
> mind charging itself
> at its own sources. (*WA* 46)

The 'Dead Worthies', in the next poem in the collection, include William Morgan, Ann Griffiths (celebrated in 'Fugue for Ann Griffiths' at the end of the collection) and the poet Robert Williams Parry, seen, poignantly, alone,

> quarrying
>
> his cynghanedd among
> Bethesda slate in
> the twilight of the language. (*WA* 47)

Again we note that uncanny, unhomely half-light. And among these isolated individuals, unyielding in their Kierkegaardian commitment, is Saunders Lewis:

> And he dared them;
> Dared them to grow old and bitter
> As he. He kept his pen clean
> By burying it in their fat
> Flesh. [. . .]
> A recluse, then; himself
> His hermitage? Unhabited

> He moved among us; would have led
> To rebellion. (*WA* 44)

For R. S. Thomas too, it seems, contemporary Wales, 'Bosworth blind', provides no home; maintenance of the pure vision of 'the true Wales of my imagination' requires something closer to the reclusive detachment of the hermitage.

Chapter III
Aberdaron

In 1972 R. S. Thomas finally escaped his post as vicar at Eglwys-fach and became vicar of Eglwys Hywyn Sant, Aberdaron, at the windswept tip of the Llŷn peninsula; the twelfth-century church is virtually at the land's edge and, when the tide is high, filled with the sounds of the sea. Across the fast-running strait is Ynys Enlli, Bardsey, an ancient site of Christian pilgrimage. The Thomases had had contacts with the area for some years; it was a place crossed at certain times of the year by large flocks of migratory birds and Thomas, an avid birdwatcher, had visited Aberdaron and Enlli with his friend, the naturalist William Condry, since the 1950s. Thomas also became friendly with the three Keating sisters who lived in the nearby Jacobean house at Plas-yn-Rhiw; he and his wife spent holidays in a cottage in the grounds. Ultimately, the sisters offered them the tenancy of another cottage, Sarn-y-Plas, and it was to this 500-year-old cottage – with its magnificent view across the bay at Porth Neigwl – that Thomas and Elsi were to move on his retirement from the church in 1978.[67] The move from Eglwys-fach almost inevitably brought a change in Thomas's imaginative concerns and, thus, in his poetry:

> I made some sort of break in my poetry coming to Aberdaron. I had a sort of feeling that I'd more or less said what I wanted to say about the farmers and the Welsh hill country and making poems out of the Welsh problem and as the very marked character of the Llŷn Peninsula began to impinge on me, I became conscious of the sea all around me, geological time, the pre-Cambrian rocks, and I began to go off in a slightly different direction.[68]

This is not of course to say that Thomas ceased entirely to write poetry about Wales and the threat to its identity: a number of new and, as we have seen, often bitter poems on these themes were collected, along with his nationalist poems of the 1960s, in *Welsh Airs* in 1987. But most of his interventions on the political situation in Wales were now expressed in prose, and primarily in Welsh, urging the Welsh-speaking Welsh to be aware of their situation and hold true to their heritage.

At Aberdaron R. S. Thomas could at last live his life in and through the Welsh language, and his comment that 'it was like a return home' (*MS* 15) is a telling one in the context of our present discussion: the world of Aberdaron seems to have felt somehow more 'real', a word he uses several times in the *South Bank Show* interview. However, while the locality was Welsh-speaking, there were English residents and the annual influx of tourists from England, and thus Thomas had still to conduct some services in English. At the same time, living much of his everyday life through the medium of Welsh seems to have made him all the more aware of the fact that he could only write poetry in his native tongue, English: 'The conflict was more acute, although it was too late to do much about it' (*A* 77).

The period of the move to Aberdaron not only saw a shift in the subject-matter of R. S. Thomas's poetry but also the beginnings of significant changes in verse technique. While the creative use of enjambement, the break of syntax across the movement between lines, had been a feature of Thomas's work since the 1950s, this becomes more overt in the period of *H'm* (1972), along with new developments such as radically irregular line indentation. Several critics responded negatively to these developments in *H'm*, seeing the poems as manifesting, in the words of Sam Adams, an 'under-developed sense of form [. . .] Occasionally one wonders what logic of sound or sense prompts him to break a line at a particular point'; John Wain found the 'flight from form' to be 'depressing' and mourned the loss of Thomas's 'beautiful sense of rhythm and sound'.[69] In a later interview Thomas confirmed that John Barnie was 'correct' in suggesting that this change of style in some poems owed something to the work of the American poet William Carlos Williams, the new forms 'being apter for new subject matter and new thinking'.[70] In fact, as David Lloyd has recently demonstrated, Thomas's response in his later poetry to his reading of Williams goes beyond syntactical experiment and includes such characteristic devices as the exclamatory opening line which suggests that the poem is a response to some preceding debate or question: 'Why no! I never thought other than / That God was that great absence / In our lives [. . .]' ('Via Negativa', *H'm* 16).[71] But it is the way Williams's work showed Thomas the possibilities of exploiting the play between syntax and line that is the most important aspect of the Welsh poet's response to the American; Lloyd points to 'the calculated un-folding of clauses down the stanza and down the poem', as in 'The River':

> And the cobbled water
> Of the stream, with the trout's indelible
> Shadows that winter
> Has not erased – I walk it
> Again under a clean
> Sky with the fish, speckled like thrushes,
> Silently singing among the weed's
> Branches. (*H'm* 23)

The sinuous movement of the sentence across the line breaks requires repeated revaluation and qualification on the part of the attentive reader; the full stop – and full meaning – is delicately, and disconcertingly, deferred. David Lloyd refers to the 'de-stabilizing and defamiliarizing of the poetic line' in such poems; indeed, the tentative, seemingly uncertain, movement of the verse can be seen as an apt means of dramatizing the poet's uneasy meditations on the physical and spiritual universe he inhabits in the later poetry: strange, uncertain, *unheimlich*.

Nor was Carlos Williams the only American poet that Thomas had been reading; indeed his study of American poetry seems to have begun in the late 1950s. In 'A Time for Carving', a BBC radio broadcast in 1957, Thomas discusses American writers' firm sense of national identity – 'the world is full enough of déracinés, God knows, and it is no small blessing this sense of belonging' – and he compares it to the Welsh writer in English.[72] Thomas makes reference to Whitman, Frost, Marianne Moore, Archibald MacLeish, Allen Tate and John Crowe Ransom, as well as to critics like Philip Rahv, Van Wyck Brooks and F. O. Mathiessen; his *Penguin Book of Religious Verse* (1963) includes work by Frost, Ransom, Whitman, Robinson Jeffers and Wallace Stevens. Thomas's awareness of more contemporary American poetry was fostered by his contact with the group of critics and poets associated with the journal *Critical Quarterly*, one of whose editors, A. E. Dyson, was based in the English Department at what was then the University College of North Wales, Bangor. Thomas's poetry appeared in the journal's second volume in 1960. Thereafter, his poems appeared regularly, both in *Critical Quarterly* itself and in the annual pamphlet selections which the journal published, alongside not only work by, for example, Philip Larkin, Ted Hughes and Thom Gunn, but also American poets like Sylvia Plath, Robert Lowell, Anne Sexton and Adrienne Rich, poets who offered new and direct ways of exploring and expressing personal feeling. While Thomas was never a 'confessional poet', the bleak moods we have noted in poems like 'Welsh Border' – 'It is a dark night [. . .] The real fight goes on / In the mind; protect me, / Spirits, from myself' – sometimes seem to inhabit a world not dissimilar to that of, for example, Lowell's 'Skunk Hour'.[73]

The opening poem of *H'm*, 'Once', immediately sets the tone for many of the poems which follow in the volume:

> God looked at space and I appeared,
> Rubbing my eyes at what I saw.
> The earth smoked, no birds sang:
> There were no footprints on the beaches
> Of the hot sea, no creatures in it.
>   [. . .] and in the late morning
> You, rising towards me out of the depths
> Of myself. I took your hand,

> Remembering you, and together,
> Confederates of the natural day,
> We went forth to meet the Machine. (*H'm* 1)

If the speaker can be seen as Adam, meeting his Eve, the scene appears to be less that of the original Creation than some kind of re-Creation ('Remembering you' and, earlier, 'As though born again') after some catastrophic event; this is not Adam and Eve in the Garden but in some scorched Waste Land (Eliot's poem is echoed at several points). They do not respond to God, but immediately go off to seek the adversary with whom God battles repeatedly in this collection: the Machine. In some ways, as critics have pointed out, Thomas's technique in these sardonic, black-humoured, cartoon-like poems echoes the mythic-cartoon poems which Thomas's *Critical Quarterly* fellow-contributor Ted Hughes was publishing in this period. (They had almost certainly met at the journal's regular summer schools. *Crow* itself was published in 1970, though the poems had been appearing in magazines for some time before that.) The God in the work of both poets is at times ineffectual:

> God tried to teach Crow how to talk.
> "Love," said God. "Say, Love."
> Crow gaped, and the white shark crashed into the sea [. . .]
> ('Crow's First Lesson')[74]

> What is this? said God. The obstinacy
> Of its refusal to answer
> Enraged him. ('Echoes', *H'm* 4)

> God secreted
> A tear. Enough, enough,
> He commanded, but the machine
> Looked at him and went on singing. (*H'm* 36)

Elsewhere, in frustrated rage at his creation, God inflicts his vengefulness:

> And God thought: Pray away,
> Creatures; I'm going to destroy
> It. The mistake's mine,
> If you like. I have blundered
> Before [. . .] ('Soliloquy', *H'm* 30)

While sometimes He seems merely illogical and spiteful:

> And God said, I will build a church here
> And cause this people to worship me,
> And afflict them with poverty and sickness
> In return for centuries of hard work
> And patience. ('The Island', *H'm* 20)

The nature of God, or of 'ultimate reality',[75] and the nature of his own relation to that God is the central theme of Thomas's later poetry. The God of *H'm* is essentially a parody of the god that humankind has created in its own image, the anthropomorphized god who can be addressed directly as 'Lord', 'King', 'Father', a being to whom supplication can be made and yet who can in response to the world's suffering and pain seem, in the human terms in which he has been constructed, illogical and cruelly indifferent.

God's adversary, the Machine, seems as indestructible as Hughes's Crow, but whereas Crow seems to represent a determined and ineradicable natural energy, Thomas's Machine represents the life-denying capacity of the mechanical. Such attitudes, of course, were not new in Thomas's work: at Manafon, Cynddylan on his new tractor had become 'part of the machine / His nerves of metal and his blood oil' ('Cynddylan on a Tractor', *AL* 16), deaf to the sound of the birds. But the Machine in Thomas's poetry does not only refer to actual machines; it represents the industrial and technological processes by which our modern world is run, and the materialistic, commercial attitudes which are the result. Ultimately the Machine is Thomas's shorthand for the mechanical, unimaginative/stereotypical thinking of globalized consumerism, in which the individual becomes merely a unit of production and consumption. 'The main criticism is that the machine is de-humanising', commented Thomas in an interview.[76] Moreover, if it is in the natural world that the imagination is most active, then exile from the natural life to the industrial, commercial, urban world of the Machine involves not only a dulling of the capacity in human beings to feel for themselves *as* individual selves, but also a loss of the human capacity to imagine; since it is for Thomas the imagination 'which is the highest means known to the human psyche of getting into contact with the ultimate reality', the world of the Machine thus represents a loss of the human capacity to apprehend the Divine.[77] A life governed by the Machine thus represents for the poet a life which alienates the individual not only from his/her unique, imaginative and authentic self but from God: a life which is one of division and disintegration rather than the wholeness, the 'at-homeness', for which Thomas has been seeking.[78]

That loss of the natural world is mourned most poignantly perhaps in 'Gone?' (F 34), an elegy for 'Prytherch country'. Any sense of attachment to the land, and all that it meant in the earlier poetry, is indeed gone:

> Nothing to show for it now: hedges
> uprooted, walls gone, a mobile people
> hurrying to and fro on their fast
> tractors; a forest of aerials [. . .]

And the televisions attached to those aerials again encourage the construction of merely conformist selves:

> They copy the image
> of themselves projected on their smooth
> screens to the accompaniment of inane
> music.

That word 'smooth' repeatedly signals in R. S. Thomas's later poetry the individuality-denying presence of the machine world:

> The machine is
> our winter, smooth
> as ice glassing
> over the soul's surface. ('Winter', *MHT* 69)

H'm itself at several points evokes an existence in which the human, and the humane, are exiled in a mechanical world of frantic and mind-numbed consumerism:

> The tins marched to the music
> Of the conveyer belt. A billion
> Mouths opened. Production,
> Production, the wheels
>
> Whistled. Among the forests
> Of metal the one human
> Sound was the lament of
> The poets for deciduous language. ('Postscript', *H'm* 22)

In the bleak but poignant final poem of the volume, humanity is trapped in a dodgem car at a nightmarish Vanity Fair, a life of money and mechanical responses :

> This is mankind
> Being taken for a ride by a rich
> Relation. The responses are fixed:
> Bump, smile; bump, smile. And the current
>
> Is generated by the *smooth* flow
> Of the shillings [. . .]
> But where he should be laughing
> Too, his features are split open, and look!
> Out of the cracks come warm, human tears.
> ('The Fair', *H'm* 37, my italics)

At times there is perhaps a touch of *Schadenfreude*; while Thomas cannot entirely escape the modern world at Aberdaron, he can for the most part live his life according to more natural rhythms. Thomas carefully juxtaposes 'Postscript' with, on the facing page, 'The River', already quoted, with its vision of a natural world of flowing water and 'a clean sky' and the poet at one with his world, 'letting the stream / Comb me, feeling it fresh / In my veins' (*H'm* 23). There are indeed at times in the collection a sense of the possibility of being at home, domestically and spiritually, and of being in touch with a wider reality:

> [. . .] eternity
> Is here in this small room,
> In intervals that our love
> Widens; and outside
> Us is time and the victims
> Of time [. . .] ('The Hearth', *H'm* 18)

But even at Aberdaron, such moments of at-homeness are fleeting. Thomas's reflections on the nature of his new environment at times stirred afresh the fundamental insecurities that we have been considering:

gazing on the pre-Cambrian rocks in Braich y Pwll, R.S. realised that he was in contact with something that had been there for a thousand million years. His head would spin. [. . .] On seeing his shadow fall on such ancient rocks, he had to question himself in a different context and ask the same old questions as before, 'Who am I?' and the answer now came more emphatically than ever before, 'No-one'.

(*A* 78)

The sheer scale of his surroundings at Pen Llŷn, while a liberation from the frustrations of Eglwys-fach, takes his imagination in new and unsettling directions: 'I became aware out on the peninsula of the wide skies, the starry sky at night, and the ocean around me, and this naturally led me into more contemplation of the universe'.[79] That star-filled darkness, unpolluted by city lights, provides both a backdrop to much of the later poetry and a focus for Thomas's own meditation on the nature of being. The mind can reach towards reassurance:

> Every night
> is a rinsing myself of the darkness
>
> that is in my veins. I let the stars inject me
> with fire, silent as it is far,
> but certain in its cauterising
> of my despair. ('Night Sky', *F* 18)

Other reflections on the night sky, 'the illuminated city / above him', are more profoundly ambiguous:

> All that brightness, he thinks,
>
> and nobody there! I am nothing
> religious. All I have is a piece
> of the universal mind that reflects
> infinite darkness between points of light.
>
> ('The Possession', *F* 33)

As Ben Astley has pointed out in his examination of the funda-mental ambivalences of this poem, the poet

> leaves us pondering the nature of man and the universe. He gives us a diction of despair ('emptiness', 'nobody there', 'nothing') starkly juxtaposed with moments of hope ('illuminated city', 'points of light'). His final image 'infinite darkness between points of light', allows us some understanding of the problem of being a man of faith [. . .] how to possess (or be possessed by) a faith beyond sensible experience.[80]

R. S. Thomas rarely made marks or notes in the margins of the books he read, but at one point in his copy of Pascal's *Pensées* he has drawn a firm line alongside the following passage, an annotation which seems to have striking resonance in the present context:

> I know not who put me into the world, nor what the world is, *nor what I myself am.* [. . .] I see those frightful spaces of the universe which surround me, and I find myself tied to one corner of this vast expanse, without knowing why I am put in this place rather than in another, nor why the short time which is given me to live is assigned to me at this point than at another of the whole eternity which was

before me or which shall come after me. I see nothing but infinites on all sides, which surround me as an atom, and as a shadow which endures only for an instant and returns no more.[81]

We noted earlier in our discussion Thomas associating such experiences of uncertainty of identity fleeing 'to the sanctuary of his mirror for re-assurance / that he is still there, challenging the eyes / to look back into his own and not / at the third person over his shoulder' ('Roles', *EA* 12); such confrontations with his mirror image recur almost obsessively at times in the poetry from the late 1970s onwards, and 're-assurance' is almost never the result:

> What was the mirror
> he looked in? Over his shoulder
> he saw fear, on the horizon
> its likeness. (*WI* 17)

In 'Looking Glass' (*EA* 40) the poet seeks to consider himself without the eyes of his mirror image looking disturbingly, challengingly, back at him:

> There is a game I play
> with a mirror, approaching
> it when I am not there,
> as though to take by surprise
>
> the self that is my familiar. It
> is in vain.

While the 'game' itself is a measure of the grip which such reflections (a predictable pun which Thomas uses repeatedly) on the nature of his identity have upon him, that 'familiar' resonates with meaning: what we see when we look in a mirror is something with which we are familiar, see every day. But, stared at intently, it can start to take on a sense of 'otherness', take on the attributes of a 'familiar' in the sense of a sinister attendant spirit. We are, clearly, back in the realm of Freud's essay on 'The Uncanny', where that which is 'homely' can be intimately related to that which is 'unhomely', the sense of dread arises precisely from, we recall, 'a peculiar commingling of the familiar and unfamiliar'. Freud, as we have noted, specifically points to the 'uncanny effect' of catching sight of one's own 'double' in a reflection.[82]

The recurrence of this mirror motif is a powerful indicator of the fact that, while Thomas may have found himself in a Welsh-speaking community at Aberdaron, his sense of being unhomed, of not being at one with the world around him, or indeed with himself, was undiminished. Thomas may not have been familiar with Freud's notions of the uncanny, but, as Katie Gramich suggests, it is unlikely that he was unaware of the way in which Freud took up the Narcissus myth to explain 'pathological conditions of self-obsession and self-love'.[83] The myth recurs in Thomas's later poetry, in conjunction with the image of the mirror and the reflecting pool. In 'A Life' (*EA* 52), perhaps the most lacerating of the self-portraits which, not insignificantly in this context, appear in Thomas's work from 'Judgment Day' onwards ('Lord, breathe once more / On that sad mirror', *T* 20), the protagonist is 'A Narcissus tortured / by the whisperers behind / the mirror', the inner voices whispering of his own inadequacies. Thomas's Narcissus is an emblem of self-doubt, of tortured self-dissatisfaction, a figure, as Gramich points out, not of self-love but, in the words of Karl Abraham, one of those who developed Freud's ideas, a figure who represents a self that is 'fundamentally [. . .] lonely and deprived of a secure base'.[84] In the poem which gives Thomas's final volume its title, 'The furies are at home / in the mirror' but the self can see no calm, secure home; the mirror and its ambiguous familiar becomes

> a chalice
>
> held out to you in
> silent communion, where gaspingly
> you partake of a shifting
> identity never your own. (*NTF* 31)

The desperation ('gaspingly') is a measure of the depth of the insecurity.

It was presumably his contemplation of the vastness of the starry night sky at Aberdaron and the sense of the universe beyond it that he stared up into that took Thomas's mind, and his poetry, in an unexpected new direction. As we have seen, Thomas's antipathy to 'the Machine', to the ways in which technology and what he saw as mechanical ways of thinking ultimately constrain the human mind, became a more central theme in his thinking and writing: 'So many times I have raised / the receiver, listening to / that smooth sound that is technology's / purring' ('Calling', *EA* 31, and again we register that adjective). While, as Ned Thomas has pointed out, the vocabulary of science and technology is present in Thomas's poetry almost from the beginning – 'Frost's cruel chemistry', 'time's geometry', 'the embryo music dead in his throat' – such registers have usually had, not unexpectedly, negative connotations. Ned Thomas argues that the poet's attitude towards humanity's aspiration to know the universe scientifically, and to control it, ultimately derives from the viewpoint of traditional Christian theology, man's aspiration to power which is ultimately God's.[85] It is an attitude that leads to division from God's way and, again, to lack of unity between the human and the natural world. Ned Thomas points to the poet's reference to 'Plato's solitary mind' (echoing Milton's Adam and Eve cast out of Eden for eating of the Tree of Knowledge: 'Through Eden took their solitary way'); in 'Pre-Cambrian' (*F* 23) the whole tradition of Western rational thought is seen as responsible for the possibility of the ultimate human disaster: 'Plato, Aristotle, / all who furrowed the calmness / of their foreheads are responsible / for the bomb'. At Aberdaron, staring up into the starlit skies, Thomas was aware that science was enabling humans to begin to reach out into space – men had stood on the moon in 1969 – and the registers and imagery of such exploration repeatedly enter his poetry in the 1970s and 1980s:

> For me now
> There is only the God-space

into which I send out
my probes. [. . .]
    And astronaut
on impossible journeys
to the far side of the self
I return with messages
I cannot decipher [. . .]
       ('The New Mariner', *BHN* 99)

Resting in the intervals
of my breathing, I pick up the signals
relayed to me from a periphery I comprehend.
       ('Night Sky', *F* 18)

At one level this new register and set of images reflected a specific poetic concern: in a radio interview to mark his seventieth birthday in 1983, he commented: 'It seems to me a disaster if we cannot make poetry which is of interest to a scientific techno-logical age. If we really have to leave a last developing body of knowledge and vocabulary out of our poetic workshop, it seems to me, there is no future for poetry.'[86]

At the same time, however, this was not a mere change of technique; a more profound shift was taking place in Thomas's thinking and this seems to have come from his reading, probably in the early 1980s, in contemporary writing about science, in particular the work of Paul Davies and Fritjof Capra. There he found a different approach to scientific thinking about the universe. In his *God and the New Physics* (1983), Davies, a professor of theoretical physics, argues that the facts about the universe which physics was discovering, in the decades following the proposition of the theory of relativity and the development of quantum theory, 'seemed to turn commonsense on its head and find closer accord with mysticism than materialism'; research on, for example, subatomic particles such as quarks and leptons and 'the fundamental forces that operate between them' was leading scientists not only to an unexpectedly holistic vision of the forces active in the processes of life but to a sense of the essential harmony and beauty of these processes.[87] Davies goes as far as to claim finally that 'science offers a surer path than religion in the search for God'. (Again, Thomas's marginal annotation is not extensive but is at times revealing, and relevant to our present discussion: at the opening of his chapter on 'The Self', Davies asserts that 'Each of us has buried deep within our consciousness a strong sense of personal identity' and that, though we grow and change, 'through it all we never doubt that we are the same person'. Thomas underlines 'Each', 'never doubt' and 'same person' and this is reinforced by firm question marks in the margin.) Fritjof Capra, another academic physicist, had come to related conclusions, albeit by a different route: he had been struck by the ways in which the universe being revealed by the theories of the new physics was strikingly similar to the holistic religious vision of Eastern religions, of Hinduism, Buddhism and Taoism, and indeed to perceptions found 'to some degree in all mystically oriented philosophies'.[88] This new scientific vision Capra sees as transcending the division between matter and spirit which has been fundamental to Western scientific thinking since Aristotle. For Davies and Capra, the new physics is a science not of human self-assertion, but of genuine and fundamental exploration; by 1981 Thomas was asserting:

> Pure science in its contemplation of the structures of the universe and the mystery of space and time, all these things are religiously orientated, it seems to me. I see no contradiction between science as such and a belief in God. It is only the machine and the use to which it is being put and technology, and some of the uses to which it's being put that seem to me to stand between man and God.[89]

Thomas makes a crucial distinction: between the material *application* of scientific thinking, the world of technology (epitomized by the RAF jets which used the Llŷn coastline as a training ground; Thomas refers to them repeatedly in interviews) towards which his hostility remains uncompromising, and 'pure science' which approaches the universe with something more akin to imaginative awe:

The new knowledge, physics especially, has reduced matter to a state of thin vapour like a current that connects two electric charges. The physicists came to see how amazing the universe is in which we live, and the tricks that time and space can play. Behind the atoms were found smaller particles, and behind those, others still smaller. [. . .] Therefore when I stand at night and look towards the stars, and think of the galaxies that stretch one after the other to oblivion, while remembering that it is all within finite space that is still expanding, I am not a dreamer belonging to the old primitive lineage of Llŷn, but someone who, partaking of contemporary knowledge, can still wonder at the Being that keeps all in balance. ('Blwyddyn yn Llŷn', A 145)[90]

Thus, the scientists' search for meanings is aligned to the poet's search for that Being who is the original source of this mysterious, reason-defying universe:

> I think he sits at that strange table
> of Eddington's, that is not a table
> at all, but nodes and molecules
> pushing against molecules
> and nodes. [. . .]
>   And I would have
> things to say to this God
> at the judgement, storming at him,
> as Job stormed, with the eloquence
> of the abused heart. But there will be
> no judgement other than the verdict
> of his calculations, that abstruse
> geometry that proceeds eternally
> in the silence beyond right and wrong. ('At It', F 15)

Implicit again, as in *H'm*, is a whole argument against God as an anthropomorphized being, an entity at whom one can 'storm' in anger, as at the illogicality and unfairness of another human being; such an anger, and indeed such a construction of God, is one based on human logic, the very logic of which the scientists themselves are confronting the inadequacy. God in these poems is associated with 'the mystery / at the cell's core, and the equation / that will not come out' ('The Gap', F 7). This is not a

God who can be addressed, or stormed at, or even prayed to in the traditional intercessory way; He/It (the inadequacies of human language to encompass 'ultimate reality' is a central theme in the later poetry)[91] can only be detected by the sometimes minute evidence of His having been present, evidence that is as likely to be detected by the scientist as the priest:

> Never known as anything
> but an absence, I dare not name him
> as God. Yet the adjustments
> are made. There is an unseen
> power, whose sphere is the cell
> and the electron. We never catch
> him at work, but can only say,
> coming suddenly upon an amendment
> that here he has been. ('Adjustments', *F* 29)

Ultimately, coming to a mature understanding of what 'God' means is 'to leave the fireside / with its tales, / the burying of the head / between God's knees' ('One Life', *MHT* 56). God is nothing so domestic or so personal; growing up, it seems:

> [. . .] is to perceive
> that knowledge of him comes
> from the genes' breaking
> of an involved code,
> from the mind's parallel
> at-homeness with missile and scalpel.

However, the sense of 'at-homeness' with the complexity of the way God is manifested in the human world in this poem of the 1990s is far from evident in the poetry of the two decades which precede it, a poetry of search and longing: 'I modernise the anachronism / of my language, but he is no more here / than before' ('The Absence', *F* 48).

To de-domesticate God, to reject the anthropomorphized personal God to whom one can make requests and from whom one can seek answers, is one thing; but having posited a being/existence/

process who/which underlies the basic processes of the universe, how can one be sure that that being in fact exists at all? And how can one come to know Him/It? In the 'adjustments [that] are made' in the 'cell and the electron', one may sense evidence of 'His' work, but, even here:

> Never known as anything
> But an absence, I dare not name him
> as God. ('Adjustments', F 29)

Again, language is not adequate to the task; there is no adequate signifier for that which the writer seeks to signify. As Ben Astley has pointed out, in Thomas's poetry of the 1970s and 1980s, he even plays with the incapacity of language to *be* precise, to signify securely, at the outer limits of human speech, with on occasion at least two possibilities held in tension in the 'free-play of the sign'. One way in which this tension shows itself is in Thomas's recurrent punning, puns which are not merely amusing wordplay, but frequently serious manifestations of ambivalence and duality of meaning.[92] In 'Abercuawg', 'An absence is how we become surer / of what we want' (F 26); sureness is one thing, but we don't just 'want' in the sense of 'desire' or 'require': we also 'want' in the sense of 'lack'. And yet so intense, so almost-tangible, is this lack, this sense of absence, that the signification of the terms themselves again becomes insecure:

> It is this great absence
> that is like a presence, that compels
> me to address it without hope
> of a reply. It is a room I enter
>
> from which someone has just
> gone, the vestibule for the arrival
> of one who has not yet come. ('The Absence', F 48)[93]

God's elusive absence/presence haunts the poems of the 1970s, sometimes in moments not of anguish but in moments of moving quietness, even of beauty. 'Sea-Watching' (*LS* 64) in a sense puns across two aspects of Thomas's life, as priest and as birdwatcher: the elusive God is like the elusive 'rare bird', as, with the poet's attentive scanning, the lines move and shift like the ebb and flow of the sea, almost inviting the elusive presence to enter the space that is left between them:

> I became the hermit
> of the rocks, habited with the wind
> and the mist. There were days,
> so beautiful the emptiness
> it might have filled,
>   its absence
> was as its presence; not to be told
> any more, so single my mind
> after its long fast,
>   my watching from praying.

Again we notice that uncanny half-light, as well as the poet's hermit-like isolation.

Indeed, in God's ambiguous absence isolation frequently darkens into loneliness in these volumes. 'The Word' (*LS* 3) begins abruptly 'A pen appeared, and the god said: / "Write what it is to be / man"'; the narrator hesitates, then 'letters / took shape on the page's / blankness, and I spelled out // the word "lonely"'. It is the judgement not only of the narrating protagonist, however, but 'of all those waiting at life's / window, who cry out loud: "It is true"'. For Thomas in this mood a sense of aloneness, of 'unhomedness', is part of the human condition. In 'Poste Restante' (*LS* 13), the poet , as in several early poems, is alone in his church, but now the mood seems all the more grim. The place is sinking 'to its knees', not in prayer but in neglect and decay. The elements of the mass lie 'cold and unwanted / by all but he'; not even two or three are any longer gathered together in communion here. The atmosphere is curiously dreamlike, with again an eerie 'raw light on the hill' and, almost inevitably, the protagonist glimpses

[. . .] his face
staring at him from the cracked glass
of the window, with the lips moving
like those of an inhabitant of
a world beyond this.

Here is no abiding home, it seems, but this whole 'poste restante' epistle is addressed to the uncertain future, a fragile message in a bottle to a time in which the Machine may have triumphed, the Cross ground 'into dust / under men's wheels', or in which, just possibly, it may shine out to 'a new era'. In 'The Porch' (*F* 10) the narrator, again in winter, with 'the moon rising', is alone at his church and is 'driven / to his knees and for no reason / he knew'; he kneels 'for an hour' not in prayer but looking 'out on a universe / that was without knowledge of him'. It is a deeply ambiguous scene: there is an acute awareness of aloneness and of the otherness of the natural universe ('an owl screamed') and yet also a curious residual sense of awe, of reverence.

Chapter IV
Retirement, Protest and Unity

The position of the poetic subject in 'The Porch', 'on that lean / threshold, neither outside nor in', is itself almost a metaphorical one, for it was in 1978, the year in which *Frequencies* was published, that R. S. Thomas retired from the Church in Wales and he and Elsi moved from the rectory in Aberdaron to Sarn-y-Plas, the small cottage they had originally leased from the Keatings (though the main house, Plas yn Rhiw, and the estate were now owned by the National Trust). He had long had misgivings about the Church's attempts to modernize the language of its worship and for him this would also be one way out: '"Let retirement be retirement indeed," he exclaimed, anticipating the changes in the liturgy of the Church' (*ERS* 102), though even here he concedes that the sea, such an inescapable presence at Aberdaron, 'revises itself over and over'. When he looks back, as he writes *The Echoes Return Slow* a few years later, there is an almost palpable sigh of relief at his escape from the routines of regular church services:

> The pretences are done with.
> The eavesdropper at the door
> is a fiction. The well-bred
>
> Amens to the formal
> orisons have begun to fade.
> I am left with the look
>
> on the sky I need not
> try turning into an expression. (*ERS* 103)

Clearly, even at Aberdaron it seems, Thomas views his role as a priest as just that, a role, a potential source of inauthenticity ('What part was he playing? Or was he just play-acting?' *ERS* 98).

Thomas's retirement freed him in other ways, too; the years that followed were those in which he became most politically active. In the early 1980s he was involved as a local organizer in the activities of the Campaign for Nuclear Disarmament (CND). He spoke at public meetings and, despite his age, took part in public demonstrations, such as that against the construction of an underground bunker in Carmarthen which was to serve as refuge for a 'regional government' in the event of a nuclear war. Gwynedd CND was in fact particularly active in the early 1980s, succeeding in persuading Gwynedd County Council to declare the county, like a number of other areas in the UK, to be a 'nuclear-free zone'. But it was his sympathy for other campaigns that brought R. S. Thomas to the attention of a public, in Wales and beyond, that had probably previously never heard of him, and certainly had not read a line of his poetry. Beginning in 1979, a group calling itself '*Meibion Glyndŵr*' (The Sons of Glyndŵr) began an arson campaign against the increasing number of houses and cottages in Welsh-speaking areas of Wales, including Llŷn, that were being bought up by English second-home owners, the effect being to raise the prices of local property beyond the reach of local young couples who wished to remain in their home districts; absentee summer homeowners also meant a significant decrease in the year-round population of some villages with a resultant decrease in local services and amenities. Despite strenuous efforts by the police, the group remained elusive and by the late 1980s there had been some 150 fires across Wales, and the offices of estate agents in Liverpool and Shrewsbury who were involved in the sale of Welsh properties were also attacked. In 1988, in a Welsh-language interview, Thomas gave support to such activities, despite the possibility that eventually someone would be killed in such an incident: 'What is one death against the death of the whole Welsh nation?'[94] The comments were widely reported and brought condemnation from the North

Wales Police, from the press (both in Cardiff and London) and from Dafydd Elis Thomas, MP, the then leader of Plaid Cymru, who compared Thomas to the French right-wing extremist Jean-Marie Le Pen: 'The attitude of blaming immigrants for economic, social and cultural changes is reminiscent of much of the obnoxious talk of the European Right.'[95] Even some in Plaid Cymru, while not necessarily supporting Thomas, felt that such comparisons were excessive, and said so in the party's own newspaper *Y Ddraig Goch*, while in *Planet* Ned Thomas wrote:

> In expressing admiration for the house-burners R. S. Thomas was not advocating a policy – he went on to say that it solved nothing – but saluting an act of resistance which dramatizes a situation. One might have expected some radical historian of the Rebecca Riots to seize upon an analogy in the arson campaign, but it took a poet to see its symbolic charge, and it took a politician – Dafydd Elis Thomas – to tell us that a nation should never listen to its poets.[96]

Challenged about his comment in an interview a few years later, and asked if it were not 'tantamount to inciting people to violence', Thomas replied:

> I don't think so. It's being quite reasonable. We have to be on the defensive in Wales because we are a small country of two and a half million people living alongside an English nation of 55 million people. When we talk about the death of one English person, we mean a physical death. But Christ said, 'Don't fear those that have the power to destroy the body, fear those that have the power to destroy both the body and the soul.' And when you're dealing with a nation, you're dealing with a spiritual concept, and there's no doubt that the soul of Wales, the identity of Wales, have been eroded and are being eroded further all the time. That is why I said that.[97]

Manifestly, Thomas was walking a perilous line between the pacifist beliefs he had held since the Second World War and his passionate, even desperate, awareness of the need to protect the Welsh language and the culture that it embodies. Here, in being willing to countenance the fact that direct action may involve fatalities, not only is he clearly moving away from the Gandhian position of passive resistance but he is seemingly willing to blur the classic distinction between physical action against property and action against people.

Two years later Thomas was again attracting hostile headlines: speaking extempore at a meeting of *Cyfamodwyr y Cymry Rhydd* (The Covenanters of the Free Welsh) in Machynlleth, the site of Glyndŵr's parliament, he advocated the placing of protest posters on English homes in Welsh-speaking areas and the removal of English-language signs; according to the *Guardian*, Thomas added that 'this must be done at night so that the authorities are prevented from finding out the extent of the opposition to the incomers.'[98] In the face of the media outcry at his comments, Thomas complained about the accuracy with which his words had been translated and reported, and insisted that 'I did not express hatred of the English, nor did I urge attacks on their property'; he added that, in an ensuing interview, 'In reply to the ritual question about the burning of cottages in Wales, I replied as usual that I was not prepared to incite others to do what I was not prepared to do myself'. At the same time he repeated his opposition to the purchase of property in Welsh areas by English incomers and condemned 'the reception by the media and their dupes of the few mildly provocative statements by me at Machynlleth'.[99]

But there was also a much less public side to R. S. Thomas's campaigning in the years after his retirement. In 1985 he became a founder member, and Secretary, of *Cyfeillion Llŷn* (The Friends of Llŷn) a group whose aims were 'To defend the Welsh language in Llŷn; to defend the interests and encourage the economy of Llŷn; to defend the environment of Llŷn'.[100] The society ultimately had a membership of over 150, with a small but active committee which met regularly. The group's initial campaign was against the building of holiday homes at Morfa Bychan by an English development company; the campaign was typical of those that were to follow: letters, from Thomas as Secretary, seeking the support of other local organizations, letters to the press, to local councils, to the developers, and to the Welsh Office. Further

campaigns were conducted against several other holiday developments and against the proposal to bury nuclear waste in the area,
as well as campaigns to protect the Welsh language in the area:
against the proposal that non-Welsh-speaking police be appointed
in Llŷn, against the use of English-only material by public bodies
like the Post Office and British Telecom and charities like the Red
Cross and the British Legion. The tone of Thomas's correspondence
could be uncompromising, and undiplomatic. When *Cyfeillion*
campaigned for the return to Llŷn of a set of prehistoric carved
stones, *Meini Penprys*, which were languishing in a dusty basement
at the Ashmolean Museum in Oxford, Thomas wrote to the
Deputy Keeper in March 1992: 'We conduct our business and
campaigning in Welsh. I write in English for your convenience
only.' (In fact cordial relations were established, the keeper visited
the area and the stones were ultimately returned.) The surviving
correspondence of *Cyfeillion Llŷn* shows a side of Thomas's
commitment to the defence of the Welsh language rather different
to the better-known image of the maker of controversial public
pronouncements; here we see a Thomas who is willing, week
after week, month after month, to expend time and energy in the
often thankless task of engaging in correspondence with public
bodies, with the Welsh Office and the Welsh Language Board,
with officials at local councils and with MPs, doggedly pressing
at an issue and not infrequently achieving a positive outcome.

But the inner life remained; retirement from the Church, and
involvement in these political activities, did not mean an end to
Thomas's spiritual explorations. In fact in many ways the contrary
was true. In a letter to a research student a few years after retiring,
Thomas writes:

I have never been very orthodox. [. . .] Language where the deity is
concerned certainly fascinates me. One of the things which least
attracts me about nonconformity is that ministers pray as though God
were listening at the key hole. [. . .] My portrayal of God in the way
you mention [presumably the kind of image of God we see in *H'm*] has
often been as a smack against bourgeois cosiness – the 'our heavenly
father' gang.[101]

But, as the poem from *The Echoes Return Slow* (p. 103) quoted above makes clear, such a conception of God was not unique to the Nonconformists; Thomas himself had had to voice the orthodoxies expected by, and accessible to, his parishioners, praying to an anthropomorphized God. But now he could step away from what were for him inadequate 'pretences'. Thomas had, as he admits in his letter, taken an unorthodox view of many aspects of Church doctrine for some years ('One small advance is that we no longer engage in witch hunts'). But now, with the constraints of regularly ministering to his flock removed, Thomas's sole concern could be with his own spiritual search. However, the casting off of the security which orthodoxy provides, to launch into the freedom of spiritual exploration, brought its own threats of disorientation:

> No piracy, but there is a plank
> to walk over seventy thousand fathoms,
> as Kierkegaard would say, and far out
> from the land. I have abandoned
> my theories, the easier certainties
> of belief. There are no handrails to grasp.
>   [. . .] Above and
> beyond there is the galaxies'
> violence, the meaningless wastage
> of force.
>   [. . .] Is there a place
> here for the spirit? Is there time
> on this brief platform for anything
> other than the mind's failure to explain itself?
>   ('Balance', F 49)

It is an extraordinary, dizzying visualization of an inner state: of personal vulnerability ('no handrails', 'this brief platform'), insecurity and, again, isolation in a vast indifferent universe; the night sky at Aberdaron is transmuted into a whole new register of anguish. In his copy of Pascal's *Pensées*, when Thomas read 'The eternal silence of these infinite spaces frightens me', he crossed out 'frightens' and wrote 'appals'.[102]

As several critics have in recent years pointed out, Kierkegaard is again a strong presence in Thomas's religious poetry in the 1970s and 1980s.[103] For Kierkegaard authentic existence for the individual is derived from faith born of constant spiritual struggle with doubt and dread in a dark world in which nothing is certain, where there are no 'objective proofs' of the reality of God:

> The Christian [. . .] has to renounce the comfort of calm assurance bolstered upon objective proofs. [. . .] Without risk there is no faith. Faith is precisely the contradiction between the infinite passion of the individual's inwardness and the objective uncertainty. If I am capable of grasping God objectively, I do not believe, but precisely because I cannot do this I must believe. If I wish to preserve myself in faith I must constantly be intent upon holding fast the objective uncertainty, so as to remain out upon the deep, over seventy thousand fathoms of water, still preserving my faith.[104]

Faith, subjective, determined and hard-won in a world of uncertainty, is the essence of authentic being for the individual, while '[. . .] objective thought translates everything into results, and helps all mankind to cheat, by copying these off and reciting them by rote'.[105] This latter is, manifestly, the unimaginative, imitative world of the Machine, the mass society of the 'Public', which denies genuine individuality because it denies the capacity for genuine thought, and doubt; it is a world which provides comfort and reassurance at the price of individual imaginative vitality: 'is man's / meaning in the keeping of himself / afloat over seventy thousand fathoms? ('Strands', *EA* 32). The depth of Thomas's imaginative and emotional response to Kierkegaard's vision is evident in the power of the vertiginous images in the poetry of the period:

> 'Life's simpleton,
> know this gulf you have created
> can be crossed by prayer. Let me hear
> if you can walk it.'
> > > 'I have walked it.

It is called silence, and it is a rope
                        over an unfathomable
abyss, which goes on and on
never arriving.'

            'So that your Amen
is unsaid. Know, friend, the arrival
is the grace given to maintain
your balance [. . .]' ('Revision', *EA* 22–3)

But the abyss of emptiness and non-meaning is always present, and God's response ambiguous. 'Threshold' is the final poem of *Between Here and Now*:

                        Ah,

        what balance is needed
        at the edges of such an abyss.
        I am alone on the surface
        of a turning planet. What

        to do but, like Michelangelo's
        Adam, put my hand
        out into unknown space,
        hoping for the reciprocating touch? (*BHN* 110)

But there is no sign of God's responding hand: facing the poem is only the blank page of the volume's endpaper.

In his contribution to the radio programme marking R. S. Thomas's seventieth birthday in 1983, Gwyn Jones commented that, while Thomas was undoubtedly 'a very fine poet', he felt that:

Many things are missing. One feels that human love is missing. The expression of the natural, kind, warm emotions of humanity are too frequently missing. Even the warmth and kindliness and love of the Christian religion seem to me to be very much underdone by R.S.

97

Thomas later commented that 'I think he's quite right to say so'.[106] Indeed, in an interview in 1999, Thomas was uncommonly frank in what he evidently saw not just as a poetic shortcoming but a personal one:

> I don't think I'm a very loving person. [. . .] I wasn't brought up in a loving home – my mother was afraid of emotion – and you tend to carry on in the same way don't you? [. . .] I'm always ready to confess the things that are lacking in me [. . .] and particularly this lack of love for human beings.[107]

One might want to argue that this is not the whole truth: there is considerable affection, especially in the poetry written at Eglwys-fach, for Iago Prytherch and the life he represents, but then one would have to concede immediately that Iago in these poems is, as we have seen, essentially an imagined figure, and 'seen' from a distance. Thomas's unambiguous attribution of the origin of his limited capacity for love is, clearly, of interest. One recalls that episode when, on the eve of his departure for university, he awoke to find his mother kissing him (*A* 36); the difficulty for Mrs Thomas, it would seem, was not feeling but its open expression, a difficulty perhaps bound up with her own up-bringing as an orphan and perhaps too with her internalizing of her perception of bourgeois self-control. What we can certainly suggest is that a self that is insecure in its identity is more likely to close protectively against the outside world, unwilling to render itself more vulnerable in the openness to others that the expression of love involves. As Graham Greene once commented, 'We cannot love others [. . .] unless in some degree we can love ourselves.'[108] Thus the search for unity of self, the search for a fulfilling state of being 'at home' with that which is beyond the self, is ultimately a search 'to find something to love'.[109] The world of the Machine, the world which R. S. Thomas portrays as that of materialist selfishness, is itself not conducive to love. In 'Casualty' (*LS* 21), the narrator is subject to the 'urgencies / of the body' in a world of girls and money: 'Every day / I went on

with that / metallic warfare in which / the one casualty is love'. The
terms in which he describes his situation are strikingly relevant
to our present argument: partaking of the things of this world
'like a Communion',

> I [. . .]
> > lost
> myself on my way
>
> home [. . .]

It is unsurprising to find Thomas adjudging himself in 'A Life'
as 'Bottom in love's school / of his class; time's reasons / too far
back to be known' (*EA* 52). What is striking, however, is the fact
that love in its various aspects, human and divine, becomes a
significant theme in *Experimenting with an Amen* especially, and
in several of the collections that followed. In 'Court Order', the
speaker, Christ, is the court fool, challenged by the king

> [. . .] to make some sport
> > with this word 'Love'. I
> did so, and was tumbled
> > into the world without
> cap and bells, to end
> > up on a hard
> shoulder, not laughing
> > with the rest who knew
> that Friday, it being April,
> > was All Fools' Day. (*EA* 42)

It is Good Friday, and the joke is on him: the court jester is about
to become the Holy Fool. God's 'sport' is to show His Love,
illogically, foolishly, by Christ's death on the Cross. The story
of the life of Christ receives remarkably little attention in R. S.
Thomas's poetry; when Christ does appear it is almost invariably
in the context of the Crucifixion. In the 1981 radio broadcast,
following a reading of 'The Musician' (*T* 19) with its vivid
evocation of the scene at Calvary, Thomas commented:

> God has given the answer to suffering in the Incarnation and the Crucifixion and Resurrection of Christ; (that the cross is the central reality in a world of time and space and it throws its shadow across the countryside, across the field of nature and across human lives). I think the Cross, the ability of God to cope with this ultimate question of the mind and the heart, his ability to do this by suffering himself lifts it out of time and space into eternity.[110]

The Cross is seen insistently in the later work as the ultimate demonstration of love defeating time and mortality: in 'Jerusalem' (*EA* 47), 'Time [. . .] chokes here on the fact / it is in high places love / condescends to be put to death'; in 'Where?' (*EA* 57) 'From the one side / history's Medusa stares, / from the other one love / on its cross'; in 'The Word' (*MHT* 71) the arms of 'the Calvary / that is our signpost' point 'in opposite directions / to bring us in the end / to the same place, so impossible / is it to escape love'. But if Christ's death can represent God's love in human terms – however incomprehensible to human logic – the full power of God's love, as Thomas tries to imagine it, is again dizzying, 'terrifying' to the exploring imagination of the lonely seeker: 'infinite / freedom in confrontation / with infinite love' ('Strands', *EA* 32). In one of Thomas's most compassionate late poems, 'Geriatric' (*NTF* 9), the poet confronts the sad, ugly realities of time's passing as he considers the bewildered inhabitants of an old people's home: 'What god is proud / of this garden / of dead flowers?' But questions of this sort, based on human logic, about suffering are swept away by the concluding vision of:

> another
> garden, all dew and fragrance
> and [. . .] these are the brambles
> about it we are caught in,
> a sacrifice prepared
> by a torn god to a love fiercer
> than we can understand.

But what of Thomas's own professed incapacity for love? It was the blunt journalistic question 'had he loved Elsi deeply?'

that brought forth Thomas's comment about his not thinking himself a very loving person. Thomas and his wife were married for over fifty years, and he nursed her through years of illness in the latter stages of her life. The relationship seems to have been as complex as Thomas's poetic response to it. Their courtship is apparently recalled in 'The Way of It' (*WI* 30); he spreads:

> the panoply
> of my feathers instinctively
> to engage her. She was not deceived,
> but accepted me as a girl
> will under a thin moon
> in love's absence as someone
> she could build a home with
> for her imagined child.

Thomas's account of the coming of that child is equally un-romantic, and self-revealing: 'the rector's wife expressed her desire to have a child. He had not thought seriously about the possibility. How can no-one be a father to someone? But so it was' (*A* 56) and the couple's only child, Gwydion, was born in 1945. One gets the clear impression of a woman of some independence – she was after all a woman whose career and reputation as an artist were developing in these years – who expected her own space, personal and creative, to be respected. Years later Thomas wrote 'There was a room / apart she kept herself in / teasing me by leading me / to its glass door, only / to confront me with / my reflection' ('Together', *R* 27); at Sarn-y-Plas, the room in which Elsi painted was at the opposite end of the cottage from where he worked. 'I was alone when I was living with her', he commented in another newspaper interview.[111] At the same time one notes that the word used is 'alone' not 'lonely'; in many respects, as I have argued elsewhere, this sense of space, the lack of emotional effusiveness would seem to have been not unwelcome to a man whose poetry suggests that he often felt his fragile sense of self to have been threatened by the emotional demands of the female.[112] This sense of a relationship of mutual respect for the identity of the other, of balanced sharing, is evident in a number of poems:

> Nineteen years now
> Sharing life's table,
> And not to be first
> To call the meal long
> We balance it thoughtfully
> On the tip of the tongue,
> Careful to maintain
> The strict palate. ('Anniversary', *T* 18)

The communion of the shared meal and the 'careful' mutual regard – in both senses of that noun – is present again in 'He and She' (*EA* 7):

> When he came in, she was there.
> When she looked at him
> he smiled. [. . .]
>
> Seated at table,
> no need for the fracture
> of the room's silence; noiselessly
> they conversed.

Fascinatingly, at the poem's conclusion Thomas draws on the nexus of images with which the reader is familiar from the poems of spiritual search:

> What was the heart's depth?
> There were fathoms in her,
> too, and sometimes he crossed
> them and landed and was not repulsed.

Again, love, like religious faith, involves risk; to become un-alone one must reach out lovingly and vulnerably, in faith and trust, beyond the self, across the dangerous fathoms. The final prose passage of *The Echoes Return Slow* again associates the poet's wife with the sea ('Both female'); this time the vulnerability of the speaker is more evident: 'Both luring us on, staring crystal-eyed over their unstable fathoms' (*ERS* 120). In the accompanying poem, however, the image is movingly transformed into an assurance of love, moving in part because of the vulnerability the image has previously expressed, and because of the faith that is now so confidently expressed:

> Am I catalyst of her mettle that,
> at my approach, her grimace of pain
> turns to a smile? What it is saying is:
> 'Over love's depths only the surface is wrinkled.'
>
> (*ERS* 121)

A few years after Elsi's death in 1991, Thomas married Betty Vernon, a vivacious Canadian woman. He and Elsi had known Betty and her husband for some thirty years, since the Thomases' time at Eglwys-fach; Betty was to be his partner until Thomas's death in 2000. Elsi's death, however, released in Thomas a depth of feeling that found expression in a sequence of poems that form a thread of quite remarkable lyrical beauty through Thomas's final two volumes, *Mass for Hard Times* and *No Truce with the Furies*, and the posthumous *Residues*. The depth and yet delicacy of feeling is perfectly caught not only in the subtle, hesitant movement between lines in these poems, but also in the way in which Elsi's physical fragility in her later years is repeatedly associated by her husband with the birds which she studied and painted with such intricate care throughout her career. 'A Marriage' has deservedly been described as a poem which is 'one of the most lyrically beautiful in the English language':[113]

> We met
>   under a shower
> of bird-notes.
>   Fifty years passed,
> love's moment
>   in a world in
> servitude to time.
>   She was young;
> I kissed with my eyes

> closed and opened
> them on her wrinkles.
>   'Come,' said death,
> choosing her as his
>   partner for
> the last dance. And she,
>   who in life
> had done everything
>   with a bird's grace,
> opened her bill now
>   for the shedding
> of one sigh no
>   heavier than a feather. (*MHT* 74)

The poem picks up the dance of death motif which recurs in *The Echoes Return Slow*, written in Elsi's last long illness, and the ravages of time are unshrinkingly registered, as we have seen, in the final poem of that sequence. In 'Still' (*NTF* 27) she has herself joined 'the autumn migration' for which she watched each year at Aberdaron. But, characteristic of these poems, there is no easy, comforting sense of her having gone, like the birds, 'southward into the burnished / and sunlit country'. Even here the nature of that 'ultimate reality', of our spiritual destination, remains a forbidding mystery: Elsi has gone 'out / into the dark, where there are / no poles, no accommodating / horizons'. The poet has loitered at the grave 'where your small bones had their nest', but he receives no simple sign to comfort him. There is just the owl, as enigmatic a presence as it is in 'Barn Owl' (*WI* 25) or 'Raptor' (*NTF* 52); and so, alone in the dark, 'I wondered'. Elsi's absence in these poems is almost palpable, as once more imagery with which we are familiar in Thomas's religious meditations is transposed into these poems of delicate intimacy:

> There is a tremor
> of light, as of a bird crossing
> the sun's path, and I look
> up in recognition
> of a presence in absence. ('No Time', *NTF* 33)

Again, the relationship is associated with looking, that play on 'regard', noted earlier, the looking which includes mutually respect-ful distance. And again too, as in the religious poems, it is love which may give access to that reality which transcends time:

> Not a word, not a sound
> as she goes her way,
> but a scent lingering
> which is that of time immolating
> itself in love's fire.

The associations of delicacy and fragility are extended in the exquisite 'Comparison' (*R* 57):

> To all light things
> I compared her; to
> a snowflake, a feather.

> [. . .] Snow
> melts, feathers
> are blown away.

> I have let
> her ashes down
> in me like an anchor.

The images of lightness and fragility, and all the ambivalences of 'let [. . .] down', resolve into the unambiguous solidity of that final image. While Thomas may not have considered himself, nor indeed have been, a man capable of expressing love easily in daily life, these poems show again the depth and tenderness of feeling of which he was actually capable, a tenderness that belies those images of dourness and austerity beloved of journalists, reviewers and, ultimately, obituary writers. As a tribute to a lost wife, these poems form a sequence unequalled since Hardy's 1912–13 poems to his first wife.

But what of that other love, love for God? Asked in 1999 'did he also *love* God?' Thomas answered:

I've been much influenced [. . .] by the American poet Robinson Jeffers, who says somewhere, 'the people who talk of God in human terms, think of that!' [. . .] No, loving God is too much of a human construct. What there must be is awe.

I feel much more at home with Wordsworth's vision of Snowdon in *The Prelude*, where he says, 'It seemed to me the type of a majestic intelligence . . . the emblem of a mind that feeds upon infinity'.[114]

The episode appears in Book 14 of *The Prelude*:

> When into air had partially dissolved
> That vision, given to spirits of the night
> And three chance human wanderers, in calm thought
> Reflected, it appeared to me the type
> Of a majestic intellect, its acts
> And its possessions, what it has and craves,
> What in itself it is, and would become.
> There I beheld the emblem of a mind
> That feeds upon infinity, that broods
> Over the dark abyss, intent to hear
> Its voices issuing forth to silent light
> In one continuous stream; a mind sustained
> By recognition of transcendent power,
> In sense conducting to ideal form,
> In soul of more than mortal privilege.[115]

This passage, in which the awe-struck Wordsworth senses some mysterious presence beyond the finite world, seems to have had particular meaning for Thomas. Thirty years earlier he had included it (as the first poem in the 'It' section) in his *Penguin Book of Religious Verse* and he refers to it again in the interview to mark his seventieth birthday, when once more he seeks to explain his understanding of the nature of God and relates the passage to more recent theological thinking:

I do like Tillich's idea of the Ground of Being, that God is not a being. I rather suspect that so many Christian – I mean we have been brought up on the Bible to believe that God is a Being, whereas the slightly more impersonal approach of Hindu thought, and Buddhistic thought for that matter, does give me the feeling that this is more what I am after. If there is any contact with an eternal reality I don't want to limit that reality to personality. It is a bit like Wordsworth's Fourteenth Book of *The Prelude* with his trip up Yr Wyddfa, Snowdon. 'It seemed to me a type of majestic intellect.' This seems to be more what I am after.[116]

Three volumes of Tillich's *Systematic Theology* were on Thomas's bookshelf when he died; while as usual annotation is sparse, the poet has firmly marked one short passage:

> However, if the notion of God appears in systematic theology in correlation with the threat of non-being which is implied in existence, God must be called the infinite power of being which resists the threat of non-being. In classical theology this is being-itself. If anxiety is defined as the awareness of being finite, God must be called the infinite ground of courage.[117]

If we relate this anxiety of being finite to that profound sense of aloneness which we have identified in Thomas, his sense of being unhomed in the world, the attraction of a notion of God as 'being itself', universal, all-pervasive, is obvious. In the late poem 'Temptation' (*R* 65), with its Tillich-like vision, the capacity to feel part of such a reality, to no longer be the lonely finite outsider is tantalizingly close:

> Not a door between us, nor a gate;
> not even the thinnest of thin
> glass. But something, something,
> so that I can neither see nor hear
> only apprehend it. [. . .]
> There are antennae within me
> aerials not palpable to the touch,
> discriminative of the transmissions
> of a being that has nothing
> to apprise me of but its presence.
> Not a being either, but being,
> that atmosphere which, when I kneel
> down, I breathe like an oxygen
> of the spirit [. . .]

The same concern with the overcoming of apartness is, of course, central to Thomas's late essay *Undod* (Unity); the very choice of subject, on being invited to give a public lecture, is itself revealing in the context of our present argument.[118] In his lecture, indeed, what we have identified as a profoundly personal need is universalized into 'man's eternal search to find unity of being' (*SP* 146). Once again, in the first section, 'The Unity of Being', he looks away from the post-Cartesian West, with its division between matter and spirit, to the East, to India – 'in spite of the plethora of gods that appealed to the common folk, there was a movement among the priests and specialists in Hinduism to bring Atman, or the self, into a state of unity with Brahman, the foundation of being' – and to China, where 'In accordance with the belief in the Tao, the emphasis is upon intuition into the order of things as a means of transcending the occasional mystical moment and of entering a permanent state of alertness to the harmony of the universe' (*SP* 147). In terms of contemporary exploration of the physical universe, Thomas again draws on Capra's *The Tao of Physics*, arguing that science, in 'shifting the emphasis away from matter as something solid to something closer to a field of force', is also moving towards a vision of the nature of being as 'a living web, which connects everything in the entire universe' (*SP* 147, 148). When Thomas turns to 'The Unity of Humanity', that unity begins with the individual: 'being at one with yourself, able to live at peace with yourself, and thus able to interact with others on the same basis' (*SP* 153). Thomas develops a vision of the natural universe remarkable for the idealism he expresses, especially when we consider the bleak, often savage, natural world that we see in the earlier poetry: now the Earth is 'a living organism', being able, for example, to maintain and control its temperature, 'as if it were a living body. If we look at it in this way, it is easy to see the Earth as an extension of God himself, as a great organism in which everything co-operates for the good of the whole' (*SP* 153). It is a vision, analogous to Lovelock's notion of *Gaia*, which implicitly contains within it, of course, a critique of those human processes, industrialism and capitalism, by which this organic unity is blighted and damaged; the earlier critiques of the deathly effects of these processes on the green world of Wales now take on more overtly universal resonance. But again it is to the individual self that Thomas returns: given this vision of an all-encompassing unity in creation,

> how can anyone keep himself separate [. . .] It is significant that losing consciousness of the self is a sign of illness in the West, but in the East it is a step on the path towards wisdom. What could be a better sign of your unity with your fellow-men than the ability to forget about yourself and to lose yourself in the feeling that you are a member of the whole organism, as God willed you to be? (*SP* 154)

But how exactly does one gain access to this transcendent unity, apprehend this 'being-itself'? Thomas's recourse is usually not to the religions of the East,[119] but to the registers, again, of Romanticism. In the Introduction to his *Penguin Book of Religious Verse*, he turns to Coleridge in his *Biographia Literaria*, where the operation of the human imagination is the 'repetition in the finite mind of the Infinite I AM'; thus, 'The nearest we approach to God, he appears to say, is as creative beings'. The poet, through his work, brings the imagination of the reader into activity, sensitizes the imaginative capacity of the individual, brings him/her 'nearer to the primary imagination [. . .] nearer to the actual being of God as displayed in action' (*SP* 48). It is thus through the operation of the imagination, the transcending of the reasoning and dissecting intellect, that one can begin to apprehend the 'ultimate reality [. . .] we call God', for 'the power of the imagination is a unifying power' (*SP* 48). For Wordsworth, Coleridge's friend and collaborator, the imagination comes into action not when the mind is actively questioning, striving for rational answers, but when the individual responds to the world in a mood of 'wise passiveness'.[120] This is the mood of 'Andante' (*EA* 61), where the natural world around us, the flowers, the clouds, the shores, requires

> no answer than the due
> we give these things that share
> the world with us, that compose
> the world: an ever-renewed
> symphony to be listened to
> admiringly, even as we perform
> it on whatever instruments
> the generations put into our hands.

It is ultimately a loving response to a unity of which one can feel a part, be at home. Nor should we lose sight of the adjective in Wordsworth's phrase – *'wise* passiveness' – this is not the self as *tabula rasa* but the self, in Christopher Morgan's acute phrase, regarding the world in a mood of 'receptive humility'.[121]

This process of seeking to intuit 'ultimate reality', or 'being-itself', has little to do with prayer as orthodoxly understood, verbal address and intercession to a God conceived of in the person of a supreme being (the God of 'the "our heavenly father" gang'). In 'The Letter' (*MHT* 77) the poet comes to the realization 'that to pray true is to say nothing': God as 'being-itself' defies 'the unreality of language', of syntax that always presumes a being as addressee. God/ultimate reality/being-itself can be intuited only in the setting aside of words, by the movement into attentive stillness and silence:

> But the silence in the mind
> is when we live best, within
> listening distance of the silence
> we call God. [. . .]

> It is a presence, then,
> whose margins are our margins;
> that calls us out over
> our own fathoms. What to do
> but draw a little nearer to such
> ubiquity by remaining still? (C 50)

With such stillness can come the transcendence of that lonely, divided self that we have seen as haunting R. S. Thomas; the image at the end of 'S.K.' (*NTF* 17) is a telling one:

> Is prayer
> not a glass that, beginning
> in obscurity as his books
> do, the longer we stare
> into the clearer becomes
> the reflection of a countenance
> in it other than our own?

At its most profound this intent stillness involves a deliberate closing down of the demands of the ego, an emptying of the self, an ignoring of the distractions of the material world. This is the *via negativa*, the negative way or 'the way of what is not', an essentially mystical tradition of apprehension that includes the author of *The Cloud of Unknowing* and the paradoxes of St John of the Cross:

> In order to arrive at possessing everything,
> Desire to possess nothing.
> In order to arrive at being everything,
> Desire to be nothing.
> In order to arrive at knowing everything,
> Desire to know nothing.[122]

Thomas's awareness of, and attraction to, this approach to the spiritual recurs throughout his later volumes, from 'Via Negativa' (*H'm* 16) onwards. It is most potently, and movingly, present, as Christopher Morgan has recently pointed out, in 'The Flower' (*LS* 25):

> I asked for riches.
> You gave me the earth, the sea,
>   the immensity
> of the broad sky. I looked at them
> and learned I must withdraw
>   to possess them. I gave my eyes
>   and my ears, and dwelt
> in a soundless darkness
>   in the shadow
>   of your regard.
>   The soul
>   grew in me, filling me
> with its fragrance.

Again the movement from line to line enacts the tentative, wondering nature of the spiritual experience, of the speaker's growing sense of the real presence, the 'regard' (again, not just a matter of looking but a 'bestow[ing] attention upon', OED) of God/being itself. The presence of that regard manifests itself not in speech or even sign but by a shift in the speaker's consciousness, a new awareness that can be described only metaphorically. The elusive absent God is sensed as 'filling' the poet's receptive darkness. (We recall that hauntingly beautiful emptiness that might have been 'filled' by God's 'presence' in 'Sea-Watching', where again the poet, hermit of the rocks, waits in attentive silence.) In such rich, fleeting moments of awareness, the sense of being an unhomed self 'outside' is transcended in Being.

Such moments *can* come unexpectedly when, the anxieties of selfhood laid aside, the self can regard the world with the imagination, lovingly, and the self knows itself as at one with some greater reality. These are T. S. Eliot's moments of the 'intersection of the timeless / With time' in *Four Quartets*:

> [. . .] the unattended
> Moment, the moment in and out of time,
> The distraction fit, lost in a shaft of sunlight,
> The wild thyme unseen, or the winter lightning
> Or the waterfall, or music heard so deeply
> That it is not heard at all, but you are the music
> While the music lasts.[123]

At such timeless moments, it seems, the self feels, paradoxically, more fully alive than as a finite being in time, feels in touch with the energy of being-itself, recurrently figured by Thomas as an endlessly self-renewing fountain of creativity:

> Let us stand, then, in the interval
> of our wounding, till the silence
> turn golden and love is
> a moment eternally overflowing. ('Evening', *NTF* 19)

'A Thicket in Lleyn' (*EA* 45) hints at another such episode: having experienced a moment in which, in the sunlight, he is surrounded by birds who do not register him as an intruder, the poet feels at one with them and afterwards reflects upon it, in Coleridgean terms, as an experience 'in time of the eternal / I AM'; again the imagination gives a fleeting intuition of a unifying reality beyond time, an awareness by which the individual should orientate his/her life:

> Navigate by such stars as are not
> leaves falling from life's
> deciduous tree, but spray from the fountain
> of the imagination, endlessly
> replenishing itself out of its own waters.

In fact, we gain a fuller, more vividly moving account of the episode, and Thomas's ensuing reflections, in an uncollected prose piece, also called 'A Thicket in Lleyn'. Approaching the thicket, quietly and attentively ('The place sighs and is still and I wait, and tune my breath to its own'), he finds it 'alive with goldcrests':

The air purred with their small wings. To look up was to see the twigs re-leafed with their bodies. Everywhere their needle-sharp cries stitched at the silence. Was I invisible? Their seed-bright eyes regarded me from three feet off. Had I put forth an arm, they might have perched on it. I became a tree, part of that bare spinney where silently the light was splintered, and for a timeless moment the birds thronged me, filigreeing me with shadow, moving to an immemorial rhythm on their way south.

Then suddenly they were gone, leaving other realities to return: the rustle of the making tide, the tick of the moisture, the blinking of the pool's eye as the air flicked it; and lastly myself. Where had I been? Who was I? What did it all mean? While it was happening, I was not.[124]

Ultimately, the uncertainty of identity in this context arises out of an experience which is in direct contrast to those earlier alienating experiences which led him to similar questions. Here 'Who was I?' arises from the shock of return from an experience where he is at one with, 'at home' in, some greater reality. In the prose account, as in the poem, Thomas recalls Coleridge:

> To him, you remember, it was the imagination which was primary: 'a repetition in the finite mind of the infinite I AM'. Is that what had happened to me? Had that infinite I announced itself in a thicket in Lleyn. [. . .] And had the I in me joined seemingly unconsciously in that announcement; and is that what eternity is? And was the mind that returned to itself but finite mind? [. . .] It was when I returned to myself that I realized that I was other, more than the experience, able to stand back and comprehend it by means of the imagination, and so by this act of creation to recognize myself not as lived by, but as part of the infinite I AM.

A sense of longing for the possibility of a richer, less isolating life is present throughout Thomas's writing, as we have seen, the yearning for a way of life where the individual may live a life more spiritually and imaginatively authentic than is possible in modern technological and consumerist society. Such a way of being is emblematized throughout Thomas's writing by those glimpses of a place that 'we [. . .] would spend / the rest of our lives looking for' ('That Place', *LS* 8): a place that is green and natural, clean and sunlit; there are usually trees, the sound of a stream nearby and, again, birdsong:

> A bird chimes
> from a green tree
> the hour that is no hour
> you know. ('Arrival', *LP* 203)

From the outset this place is located in a version of Wales; as we have noted, as early as 'The Tree' (1952) Thomas writes of the Welsh living a life of rural vitality and freedom in the age of Owain Glyndŵr, summer in the tree's branches and the sound of 'Rhiannon's birds'. Here the vision is communal, inclusive, but in the distant past. A version of the scene recurs in Thomas's remarkable prose piece 'The Mountains' (1968): '[T]here is Eden's garden, its gate open, fresh as it has always been, unsmudged by the world. The larks sing high in the sky. No footprints have bruised the dew' (*SP* 81), though we note here, even as Thomas is supposedly evoking the communal world of the *hafotai*, the scene is empty of people. In 'Again' (*NHBF* 41) the moment is a solitary one, albeit its wider human significance is registered:

> For one hour
> I have known Eden, the still place
> We hunger for. My hand lay
> Innocent; the mind was idle.

The fullest evocation of this place and the timeless vision it represents is undoubtedly that of 'Abercuawg', the lecture Thomas gave, in Welsh, at the National Eisteddfod in 1976: '[. . .] whatever Abercuawg might be, it is a place of trees and fields and flowers and bright unpolluted streams, where the cuckoos continue to sing.' (*SP* 125). It is everything which our modern urban world with its 'endless streets of modern characterless houses [. . .] from where the trees and birds and flowers have fled' is not. 'For such a place' as Abercuawg, writes Thomas, 'I am ready to make sacrifices, maybe even to die', and again, perhaps, there is a half-remembered echo of Kierkegaard:

> What matters is to find a purpose, to see what it really is that God wills that *I* shall do; the crucial thing is to find a truth *for me*, to find *the idea for which I am willing to live and die.*[125]

At one level, clearly, Abercuawg is a vision of a transfigured Wales, a version of that 'true Wales of my imagination', for which Thomas had longed since he had looked westwards from Tallarn Green, the place of a fulfilled life, of 'home'. It is the urgent, personal vision which underlies the intensity of his nationalism, the vision from which the actuality of Wales would always fall short.

But at another level the search for 'Abercuawg', as the essay gradually makes clear, is a search 'within time, for something which is above time, and yet, which is ever on the verge of being'; in other words the search becomes, again, the search for intimations of the eternal, for God/being-itself. The longing for Abercuawg is thus, as J. P. Ward has suggested, 'a desire for some primal unity'.[126] It is a place never to be arrived at, a reality never to be achieved in this world, but 'through striving to see it, through longing for it', the individual can 'succeed in preserving it as an eternal possibility' (*SP* 131). Such striving, such awareness of possibility, keeps open the channels of the imagination, keeps the self open to intimations of being-itself: 'May it not be that alongside us, made invisible by the thinnest of veils, is the heaven we seek?' ('Where do we go from here?' *SP* 120).

One of the final evocations of this sense of the possibility of wholeness of being, a transcendence of the sense of the world as *unheimlich*, comes in *No Truce with the Furies*, the final collection that Thomas himself saw through the press. Like 'Abercuawg', 'Afallon' evokes a place of visionary timelessness, deep in the Welsh imagination; the scene is by now a familiar one:

> Standing
> under the tree of man,
> our roots in the soil, we listen
> to Rhiannon's birds high
> in the branches, calling to us
> to forget time, so that the
> heart answers [. . .] (*NTF* 25)

And then we have an image, enigmatic yet vivid as a film shot, that has striking relevance to our present discussion:

> the traveller gets down
> onto a midnight platform
> and knows from the rustle
> of unseen water-
> falls he has come home.

The very title of Thomas's final volume, though, cautions us against drawing simplistic conclusions about the finality of such moments; they are elusive, fleeting. The restless search from which the poetry stems, from which it *always* stemmed, continued; the volume that contains 'Afallon' also contains 'The Lost' (*NTF* 14), a poem which, though it originates in the Welsh situation, also has resonance which is both personal and universally modern:

> 'Show us,'
> we supplicate, 'the way home',
> and they laughing hiss at us:
> 'but you are home. Come in
> and endure it.' Will nobody
> explain what it is like
> to be born lost?

When R. S. Thomas died on 25 September 2000, his passing was widely reported in the British and indeed the overseas media. Many of his obituary writers seemed more familiar with his earlier work. He was the 'Poet who hymned the hill farmers of North Wales in verse as rugged as the terrain in which they tended their sheep', his poetry was 'granite', 'bleak';[127] three of the London broadsheets used the same picture of a rather wild-haired Thomas staring somewhat intimidatingly from the door of his cottage at Sarn-y-Plas, Rhiw: he was 'formidable' and 'reclusive'. In Wales both the *Daily Post* and the *Western Mail*, despite their past condemnation of some of Thomas's public pronouncements, gave his death a coverage which might have surprised the poet by its extensiveness and its respect: 'A brave voice stilled in the land he loved', 'a poet we should be proud of'.[128] But, perhaps inevitably in a world of headlines, little real attention was paid to the unity of R. S. Thomas's work, nor to the fact that he is one of the great religious poets of the twentieth century. His is a religious poetry for our times not because of his faith – though the expression of that faith can be deeply moving – but because of his anguish and uncertainty, because of the strenuousness of his questioning and the persistence of his search for something eternal. In its lack of doctrinal conformity, it is a poetry which has resonance for many who would not consider themselves orthodox Christian believers but for whom the material values of the contemporary globalized world are insufficient.

In the last year of his life, R. S. Thomas was invited by the BBC to choose some of his favourite passages of literature for a programme in the Radio 4 series *With Great Pleasure*. As well as passages from Hardy and Wallace Stevens and several biblical passages, Thomas also chose a passage from Tolstoy's *War and Peace*; Pierre, in conversation with Prince André, is reflecting on whether he believes in a future life:

> 'You say that you cannot see the kingdom of goodness and truth on earth. Neither have I seen it: nor is it possible for anyone to see it who looks upon this life as the sum and end of all. On the earth, that is to say on this earth' (Pierre pointed to the fields), 'there is no truth; all is falsehood and evil: but in the universe, in the whole universe, truth has its kingdom; and we who are now children of the earth are none the less children of the universe. Do I not feel in my soul that I am actually a member of this vast harmonious whole? [. . .] If God and the future exist, then truth and virtue exist; and man's highest happiness consists in striving for their attainment. One must live,' said Pierre, 'one must love, one must believe that we live not merely now on this patch of earth, but that we have lived and shall live eternally there in the universe.' He pointed to the sky.

R. S. Thomas, 1914.

Drawing of R. S. Thomas by Elsi Thomas, 1939.

Mildred Eldridge ('Elsi'), 1934.

Elsi and R. S. Thomas, c.1940 (possibly taken on their wedding day).

I look out at the timeless sea
over the head of one, calendar
to time's passing, who is now open
at the last month, her hair wintry.

Am I catalyst of her mettle that,
at my approach, her grimace of pain
turns to a smile? What it is saying is:
Over love's depths only the surface is wrinkled.

'Cariad', manuscript in R. S. Thomas's hand, 1984.
(Collected as final poem in The Echoes Return Slow.)

Elsi and R. S. Thomas at Tallarn Green, 1940.

Album

My father is dead.
I who am look at him
who is not as once he
went looking for me
in the woman who was.

There are pictures
of the two of them no
need of a third hand
in hand hearts willing
to be one but not three.

What does it mean
life? I am here I am
there. Look! suddenly
the young tool in their hands
for hurting one another.

And the camera says:
Smile. There is no wound
time gives that is not bandaged
by time. And so they do the
three of them at me who weep.

'Album', manuscript in R. S. Thomas's hand.
(*Collected in* Frequencies, 1978.)

'Hump backed, gone in the middle, spindle shanked me.'
Self-portrait by Elsi Thomas, 1989.

'Latest profile of braces, shirt and pants.'
Drawing by Elsi Thomas of her husband, 1989.
(In the original sketch R. S. Thomas is wearing his trademark red tie.)

Notes

1   Jason Walford Davies, *Gororau'r Iaith: R. S. Thomas a'r Traddodiad Llenyddol Cymraeg* (Caerdydd: Gwasg Prifysgol Cymru, 2003), p. 50.
2   Barbara Prys-Williams, *Twentieth-Century Autobiography* (Cardiff: University of Wales Press, 2004), p. 123.
3   R. S. Thomas, 'Autobiographical Essay', *Miraculous Simplicity: Essays on R. S. Thomas*, ed. William V. Davis (Fayetteville: University of Arkansas Press, 1993), p. 20. Further references are included in the text (*MS*).
4   Letter to Gwyn Jones [*c*.1939]. NLW, Prof. Gwyn Jones Papers, 41/222.
5   See Thomas's letters to *Y Llan*: 'Arweinyddiaeth' (7 Mawrth 1947), 6, and 'Yr Eglwys a Chymru', (2 Medi 1949), 5. The latter is reprinted in *Pe Medrwn yr Iaith ac Ysgrifau Eraill*, ed. Tony Brown and Bedwyr Lewis Jones (Swansea: Christopher Davies, 1988), pp. 43–5.
6   John Macquarrie, *Existentialism* (London: Hutchinson, 1972), pp. 161–2.
7   Katie Gramich, 'Mirror Games: Self and M(O)ther in the Poetry of R. S. Thomas', in *Echoes to the Amen: Essays after R. S. Thomas*, ed. Damian Walford Davies (Cardiff: University of Wales Press, 2003), p. 142.
8   'Autobiography', *Wave* 7 (1973), 36–7.
9   Fiona Macleod, *Pharais* and *The Mountain Lovers* (London: Heinemann, 1927).
10 John Ormond, 'R. S. Thomas: Priest and Poet', *Poetry Wales* 7.4 (1972), 50.
11 'Maldwyn', *Pe Medrwn*, p. 47. My translation.
12 The Critical Forum: 'R. S. Thomas Reads and Discusses His Own Poems', Norwich Tapes, 1978, quoted by Sandra Anstey, 'Some Uncollected Poems and Variant Readings from the Early Work of R. S. Thomas', *The Page's Drift: R. S. Thomas at Eighty*, ed. M. Wynn Thomas (Bridgend: Seren, 1993), p. 23. Further references are abbreviated as *PD*.
13 NLW MS 20006 C. It seems likely that these six poems were those which R. S. Thomas sent to Gwyn Jones from Chirk in 1939 for publication in *The Welsh Review*. See letter to Gwyn Jones [? July 1939], NLW, Prof. Gwyn Jones Papers, 41/130. On these poems see Anstey, *PD* 23.
14 Untitled poem, *Dublin Magazine*, July–September 1940, 6.

[15] Norwich Tapes, quoted by Anstey, *PD* 28.

[16] 'clods' appears as 'clouds' in *SF*; this is changed to 'clods' in *SYT* and *Selected Poems*. 'clouds' reappears in *Collected Poems 1945–1990*.

[17] M. Wynn Thomas, 'R. S. Thomas: War Poet', *Welsh Writing in English: A Yearbook of Critical Essays* 2 (1996), 82.

[18] Norwich Tapes, quoted by Anstey, *PD* 28.

[19] Patrick Crotty, 'Lean Parishes: Patrick Kavanagh's *The Great Hunger* and R. S. Thomas's *The Minister*', *Dangerous Diversity: The Changing Faces of Wales*, ed. Katie Gramich and Andrew Hiscock (Cardiff: University of Wales Press, 1998), p. 131.

[20] Crotty, 'Lean Parishes', pp. 142, 145.

[21] *Horizon* printed Part I, II and 26 lines of Part IV. I am extremely grateful to Mr Sam Perry of the University of Leicester for drawing my attention to this earlier publication of Kavanagh's poem. Thomas's 'Homo Sapiens' appeared in *Horizon* 4.22 (1941), 232.

[22] Patrick Kavanagh, *The Great Hunger*, *Collected Poems* (London: MacGibbon and Kee, 1964) 35. Further references are included in the text (*GH*).

[23] 'Gideon Pugh', *Wales* 6 (Winter 1944–5), 47. My italics.

[24] Ormond, 'Priest and Poet' 50; J. P. Ward, *The Poetry of R. S. Thomas* (Bridgend: Seren, new. ed. 2001), p. 39.

[25] Nicholas Royle, *The Uncanny* (Manchester: Manchester University Press, 2003), p. 1. I am grateful to two of my recent doctoral students for discussion of the uncanny and the *unheimlich*: to Emma Nock for drawing my attention to Freud's essay, in her work on Graham Greene, and to Dr Fflur Dafydd for stimulating discussion of the relevance of such ideas to R. S. Thomas. Dr Dafydd's dissertation considers R. S. Thomas and the unhomely in the context of the postcolonial.

[26] Royle, *Uncanny*, p. 2.

[27] Sigmund Freud, 'The Uncanny', *Standard Edition of the Complete Psychological Works*, vol. 17, trans. James Strachey and Anna Freud (London: Hogarth, 1955), pp. 219, 220.

[28] Royle, *Uncanny*, p. 1.

[29] Freud, 'Uncanny', pp. 245–7.

[30] Royle, *Uncanny*, p. 2.

[31] *Dublin Magazine* (October–December 1949), 5.

[32] Ward, *Poetry*, p. 22.

[33] Freud, 'Uncanny', p. 234.

[34] *Wales* 1 (July 1943), 4.

[35] R. S. Thomas refers to his reading of the 'restarted *Wales*' and its 'emphasis on Welshness' in *Neb* (*A* 53). M. Wynn Thomas has pointed out the connection between Thomas's hill farmers and the notion of

the 'aboriginal Welsh' in Powys and in the writing of H. J. Fleure, the Aberystwyth anthropologist whose work was also published in *Wales*. See 'R. S. Thomas: War Poet', 87–9.

36 *Wales* 2 (October 1943), 49.

37 The rhyme translates as 'But give us to live / At the bright hem of God, / In the heather, in the heather'. On the rhyme, see *Gororau'r Iaith*, pp. 244–5. Rhys Davies's comments appear in his 'From my Notebook', *Wales* 2 (October 1943), 10–12.

38 'Replies to "Wales" Questionnaire 1946', *Wales* 6.3 (1946), 22.

39 *SP* 30. For a detailed discussion of the links between Thomas and MacDiarmid, see Fflur Dafydd, '*[A] shifting / identity never your own': The uncanny and the unhomely in the Poetry of R. S. Thomas*. (Ph.D. dissertation, University of Wales, Bangor, 2004). On the visit to Saunders Lewis at Llanfarian in 1945, see *A* 54.

40 *The Welsh Nationalist* (December 1948), 3. A. W. Wade-Evans's essay 'Anglo-Welsh' had appeared in *Wales* 6.3 (Autumn 1946), the issue in which 'Some Contemporary Scottish Writing' had appeared.

41 See, for example, 'Wales' (*SYT* 47), 'The Ancients of the World' (*SYT* 51) and 'Winter Retreat' (*SF* 28) with its allusion to the Twrch Trwyth in *Culhwch ac Olwen*.

42 'The Poet's Voice', BBC Radio Broadcast, 21 August 1947.

43 On Thomas's response to Austin Clarke, see his comments in 'R. S. Thomas in conversation with Molly Price-Owen', *David Jones Journal* (R. S. Thomas Special Issue) (Summer / Autumn 2001), 99, and *Gororau'r Iaith*, pp. 144–8.

44 'Song', *Dublin Magazine* (January–March), 1948: 3.

45 Ormond, 'Priest and Poet', 49.

46 In 'More Poetry at Large, 4', BBC Radio 3, 3 January 1975, Thomas commented, following an extract from *The Minister*: 'Well, this is probably a projection of myself rather than a true picture of the minister because Nonconformist ministers in Wales on the whole, I would say, are quite close to the people.'

47 Ben Astley, 'Iago Prytherch and the Rejection of Western Metaphysics', *Welsh Writing in English: A Yearbook of Critical Essays* 5 (1999), 104.

48 Astley, 'Iago Prytherch', p. 108.

49 Prys-Williams, *Autobiography*, p. 145.

50 Ward, *Poetry*, p. 44.

51 Freud, 'Uncanny', p. 235.

52 Freud, 'Uncanny', p. 248.

53 Ward, *Poetry*, p. 78.

54 For a fuller discussion, see Tony Brown, '"Blessings Stevens": R. S. Thomas and Wallace Stevens', *Echoes to the Amen*, pp. 112–31.

55 Christopher Morgan, *R. S. Thomas: Identity, Environment and Deity* (Manchester: Manchester University Press, 2003), pp. 14, 15.

56 Letter to Islwyn Ffowc Elis, 22 September 1952. NLW Islwyn Ffowc Elis Papers, File P1/3, Letters O-W 1952–1994. My translation. I am grateful to Dr T. Robin Chapman for drawing this letter to my attention.

57 'The Welsh Parlour', *Listener* (16 January 1958), 119. The reference to 'the real Wales' echoes, of course, the phrase he uses in his account of looking west from Tallarn Green.

58 Interview with Mr G. O. Hughes, churchwarden at Eglwys-fach, by Ian Hamilton, for *Bookmark*, BBC 2, 1986.

59 For a discussion of the allusions in 'Border Blues', see Davies, *Gororau'r Iaith*, pp. 64–73.

60 See Dafydd Elis Thomas, 'The Image of Wales in R. S. Thomas's Poetry', *Poetry Wales* 7.4 (Spring 1972), 62–3.

61 Islwyn Ffowc Elis, *Cymeriadau Cenedlaethol*, NLW Islwyn Ffowc Elis Papers (item uncatalogued). I am grateful to Dr T. Robin Chapman for drawing this text to my attention.

62 M. Wynn Thomas, *Internal Difference: Twentieth-Century Writing in Wales* (Cardiff: University of Wales Press, 1992), p. 120.

63 Quoted in Wynn Thomas, *Internal Difference*, p. 118.

64 Søren Kierkegaard, 'Diapsalmata', *Either / Or*, vol. 1, trans. David F. Swenson and Lillian M. Johnson (Princeton, NJ: Princeton University Press, 1959), p. 41.

65 'Welsh Parlour', p. 119. My italics.

66 *Internal Difference*, p. 124.

67 On Thomas and the Keating sisters, see Justin Wintle, *Furious Interiors: Wales, R. S. Thomas and God* (London: Harper Collins, 1996), pp. 315–17.

68 'The Poetry and Life of R. S. Thomas', *The South Bank Show*, prod. Melvyn Bragg, ITV, 17 February 1991.

69 Sam Adams, 'A Note on Four Poems', *Poetry Wales* 7.4 (1972), 75; John Wain, *Professing Poetry* (London: Macmillan, 1972), p. 152.

70 Ned Thomas and John Barnie, 'Probings: An Interview with R. S. Thomas', *Planet* 80 (April/May 1990), 50. The interview is reprinted in *MS* 21–46.

71 David Lloyd, 'Making It New: R. S. Thomas and William Carlos Williams', *Welsh Writing in English: A Yearbook of Critical Essays* 8 (2003), 121–40.

72 'A Time for Carving', BBC Welsh Home Service, 21 April 1957.

73 *Life Studies* (London: Faber, 1959), pp. 103–4. Lowell's setting is also 'One dark night', both poems presumably alluding to St. John of the Cross. Thomas mentions his contact with the editors of *Critical*

Quarterly in his conversation with Molly Price-Owen, 94. Sylvia Plath and Ted Hughes, like Thomas, attended the *Critical Quarterly* summer schools in Bangor and in London.

74 Ted Hughes, *Crow* (London: Faber, new ed. 1972), p. 20.

75 Ormond, 'Priest and Poet', p. 54.

76 Thomas and Barnie, 'Probings', 43.

77 Ormond, 'Priest and Poet', p. 54: 'I'm using the word imagination in the Coleridgean sense, which is the highest means known to the human psyche of getting in touch with the ultimate reality'.

78 Morgan, *Identity*, p. 111.

79 'Furrows into Silence', BBC Radio 4, 31 July 1981.

80 Ben Astley, '"Somewhere between faith and doubt": R. S. Thomas and the Poetry of Faith Deconstructed', *Welsh Writing in English: A Yearbook of Critical Essays* 4 (1998), p. 84.

81 Blaise Pascal, *Pensées* (London: Dent/Everyman, 1931), p. 55, my italics. R. S. Thomas's copy is at the R. S. Thomas Study Centre, Bangor (RSTSC). Thomas has drawn a line, with a cross/asterisk at either end, from the beginning of this passage to the end of the paragraph which concludes 'And indeed to what use in life could one put him?' (p. 56). In fact, the bulk of the passage, including the words quoted here, is in quotation marks in Pascal's text, as an example of the words of a man whom one would not 'desire to have for a friend': 'In truth, it is the glory of religion to have for enemies men so unreasonable.'

82 Freud, 'Uncanny', p. 248.

83 Gramich, 'Mirror Games', p. 141.

84 Gramich, 'Mirror Games', p. 142.

85 Ned Thomas, 'R. S. Thomas: The Question about Technology', *Planet* 92 (April/May 1992), 54–60. For an exhaustive examination of Thomas's use of scientific registers and imagery see John Pikoulis, 'The Curious Stars': R. S. Thomas and the Scientific Revolution', *Echoes to the Amen*, pp. 76–111.

86 'R. S. Thomas at Seventy', BBC Radio 3, 7 December 1983. Reprinted in M. M. J. van Buuren, *Waiting: The Religious Poetry of Ronald Stuart Thomas*, published Ph.D. thesis, University of Nijmegan, 1993, pp. 172–81.

87 Paul Davies, *God and the New Physics* (London: Penguin, 1984), pp. 220–22, 223. R. S. Thomas's copy is at the RSTSC.

88 Fritjof Capra, *The Tao of Physics* (1974; London: Fontana/Flamingo, 1983), p. 23. Thomas also read Capra's *The Turning Point: Science Society and the Rising Culture* (1982; Fontana/Flamingo, 1983). In the latter, when Capra in his chapter 'The Passage to the Solar Age' writes, 'To return to a more human scale will not mean a return to the past but, on the contrary, will require the development of ingenious

new forms of technology and social organisation' (442), Thomas has marked the passage with two firm marginal lines and written 'Llŷn'. Copy in the RSTSC.

89 'Furrows into Silence', 11.

90 Thomas's attitude to technology and the 'new science' is discussed in Morgan, *Identity*, which appeared while the present study was in preparation. See Morgan, Chs. 3 and 4.

91 See Tony Brown, 'Language, Poetry and Silence: Some Themes in the Poetry of R. S. Thomas', *The Welsh Connection*, ed. W. M. Tydeman (Llandysul: Gomer, 1987), pp. 159–85.

92 Astley 'Somewhere between faith and doubt', 77; Damian Walford Davies, '"Double-entry poetics": R. S. Thomas – Punster', *Echoes to the Amen*, pp. 148–82.

93 In the context of the theme of God as 'that great absence / In our lives' ('Via Negativa', *H'm* 16), Damian Walford Davies (172) points to the puns in 'Mischief', *NTF* 45: 'I have developed my negatives / of the divine and preserved their technicolour / in a make-believe album'.

94 *Guardian* (10 May 1988), 3. Various different translations of Thomas's words appeared in the press.

95 'Who's hiding the dragon?', *Guardian* (12 May 1988), 23.

96 'Can Plaid Survive?' *Planet* 70 (August/September 1988), 5. An HTV poll at the time showed 85% of the the people of Dwyfor expressing support for the arsonists' actions, *Guardian* (29 March 1993), 9.

97 *The Oldie* 79 (October 1995), 15.

98 '"Deface English homes, says poet", *Guardian* (17 September 1990), 3.

99 'Reflections on a Speech at Machynlleth', *Planet* 84 (December 1990/January 1991), 3–6.

100 Minute Books of Cyfeillion Llŷn, 1985–97, including the minutes kept by R. S. Thomas, 1985–93, along with correspondence, in the archives of the RSTSC. My translation.

101 Letter to Simon Barker, 21 March 1983, in Simon Barker, *Probing the God-Space: R. S. Thomas's Poetry of Religious Experience*, Ph.D. dissertation, University of Wales, Lampeter, 1991, 295.

102 *Pensées*, p. 61.

103 As well as Barker, *Probing the God-Space*, see Rowan Williams, 'Suspending the Ethical: R. S. Thomas and Kierkegaard', *Echoes to the Amen*, pp. 206–19, which cites other studies on the topic.

104 David F. Swenson and Walter Lowrie, trans., *Kierkegaard's Concluding Unscientific Postscript* (Princeton: Princeton University Press, 1941), pp. xvii, 182. See 'R. S. Thomas talks to J. B. Lethbridge', *Anglo-Welsh Review* 74 (1983), 54, '*Concluding Unscientific Postscript* [. . .] – every few years it does one good to tackle it, I suppose'.

105 *Concluding Unscientific Postscript*, p. 68.

106 'R. S. Thomas at Seventy', van Buuren, *Waiting*, 179–80; interview with Simon Barker (5 September 1984) in Barker, *Probing the God-Space*, 315.

107 'A poet who sang creation', *Daily Telegraph* 4 December 1999 [Arts Section] 1, 7.

108 Graham Greene, *A Sort of Life* (London: Bodley Head, 1971), p. 9.

109 R. S. Thomas, Introduction to *The Batsford Book of Country Verse* London: Batsford, 1961), p. 8.

110 'Furrows into Silence', 23.

111 *Independent on Sunday* (25 September 1994).

112 Tony Brown, '"Eve's Ruse": Identity and Gender in the Poetry of R. S. Thomas', *English*, 49.195 (Autumn 2000), 229–50.

113 'A poet who sang creation', 1.

114 'A poet who sang creation', 1.

115 *The Prelude*, Bk. 14, ll. 63–77.

116 'R. S. Thomas at Seventy', 178. Thomas had written to Simon Barker in similar terms earlier the same year: 'Perhaps I could say it is people like Whitehead and Tillich that appeal more, because of their attempt to distance the deity. [. . .] I am more sympathetic to Hindu and Buddhistic thought for the same reason. But I have not read widely.' Letter to Simon Barker, 9 January 1983, Barker, *Probing the God-Space*, p. 293. Referring to this letter, Barker makes the connection between Tillich and the passage from *The Prelude* and points out that Thomas also selected *The Prelude* passage when invited to contribute to *A Way with Words: Favourite Pieces Chosen by Famous People*, eds Christina Shewell and Virginia Dean (London: Sinclair Browne, 1982), Barker, *Probing the God-Space*, p. 102.

117 Paul Tillich, *Systematic Theology*, vol. 1 (Welwyn, Herts.: James Nisbet, 1953), p. 72. Copy at RSTSC.

118 'Undod' was originally delivered as the J. R. Jones Memorial Lecture at University College, Swansea, 9 December 1985.

119 Though we note his comment in a letter that 'I am tinged with Eastern ideas about religion – Tat twam asi and such like'. Letter to Simon Barker, 21 March 1983, Barker, *Probing the God-Space*, p. 295.

120 Wordsworth, 'Expostulation and Reply' (*Lyrical Ballads*, 1798); Thomas quotes the lines which include the phrase in the introduction to his *A Choice of Wordsworth's Verse* (*SP* 96).

121 Morgan, *Identity*, p. 180.

122 *The Complete Works of St. John of the Cross*, vol. 1, trans. E. Allison Peers, quoted in Helen Gardner, *The Art of T. S. Eliot* (London: Faber, 1968), p. 168. A number of scholars have written about R. S. Thomas and the

tradition of the *via negativa*. See, for example, Dewi Z. Phillips, *R. S. Thomas: Poet of the Hidden God* (Basingstoke: Macmillan, 1986), Elaine Shepherd. *R. S. Thomas: Conceding an Absence: Images of God Explored* (London: Macmillan, 1996) and Morgan, , *Identity*, pp. 173–86.

[123] T. S. Eliot, 'The Dry Salvages', *Complete Poems and Plays* (London: Faber, 1969), p. 190. In the original publication of 'The Flower', in *Planet* 18/19 (1973), 11, 'in the shadow / of your regard' appears as 'in the sunlight / of your regard'.

[124] 'A Thicket in Lleyn', *Britain: A World by Itself* (London: Aurum Press, 1984), p. 96.

[125] Quoted from Kierkegaard's *Journals and Papers* in Avi Sagi, *Kierkegaard, Religion and Existence: The Voyage of the Self* (Amsterdam: Rodopi, 2000), p. 7. Italics in *Journals and Papers*.

[126] Ward, *Poetry*, p. 96.

[127] *Times* (27 September 2000) 5, 25; *Guardian* (27 September 2000), 22.

[128] *Western Mail* (27 September 2000), 11; (29 September 2000).

Select Bibliography

A full bibliography of R. S. Thomas's writing to 1993 is to be found in John Harris (ed.), *A Bibliographical Guide to Twenty-Four Modern Anglo-Welsh Writers* (Cardiff: University of Wales Press, 1994), pp. 305–30.

Poetry

The Stones of the Field (Carmarthen: Druid Press, 1946)
An Acre of Land (Newtown, Mont: Montgomeryshire Printing Co., 1952)
The Minister (Newtown, Mont: Montgomeryshire Printing Co., 1953)
Song at the Year's Turning (London: Hart-Davis, 1955). Includes *The Minister*, selections from *The Stones of the Field* and *An Acre of Land* plus additional poems.
Poetry for Supper (London: Hart-Davis, 1958)
Tares (London: Hart-Davis, 1961)
The Bread of Truth (London: Hart-Davis, 1963)
Pietà (London: Hart-Davis, 1966)
Not That He Brought Flowers (London: Hart-Davis, 1968)
H'm (London: Macmillan, 1972)
Young and Old (London: Chatto & Windus, 1972)
Selected Poems 1946–68 (London: Hart-Davis, MacGibbon: 1973, rpt. Newcastle upon Tyne: Bloodaxe, 1986)
What is a Welshman? (Llandybïe: Christopher Davies, 1974)
Laboratories of the Spirit (London: Macmillan, 1975)
The Way of It (Sunderland: Ceolfrith, 1977)
Frequencies (London: Macmillan, 1978)
Between Here and Now (London: Macmillan, 1981)
Later Poems 1972–1982 (London: Macmillan, 1983)
Ingrowing Thoughts (Bridgend: Poetry Wales Press, 1985)
Experimenting with an Amen (London: Macmillan, 1986)
Welsh Airs (Bridgend: Poetry Wales Press, 1987)
The Echoes Return Slow (London: Macmillan, 1988)
Counterpoint (Newcastle upon Tyne: Bloodaxe, 1990)

Mass for Hard Times (Newcastle upon Tyne: Bloodaxe, 1992)
No Truce with the Furies (Newcastle upon Tyne: Bloodaxe, 1995)
Residues, ed. M. Wynn Thomas (Tarset: Bloodaxe, 2002)

Collected Poems, 1945–1990 (London: Dent, 1993)
R. S. Thomas, ed. Anthony Thwaite (London: Dent/Everyman, 1996)
R. S. Thomas: Selected Poems. Penguin Modern Classics (Harmondsworth: Penguin, 2004)
Collected Later Poems 1988–2000 (Tarset: Bloodaxe, 2004)

Prose

R. S. Thomas: Selected Prose, ed. Sandra Anstey (Bridgend: Poetry Wales Press, 1983; rev. ed. 1995)
Neb (Caernarfon: Gwasg Gwynedd, 1985) (autobiography)
Pe Medrwn yr Iaith ac Ysgrifau Eraill, ed. Tony Brown and Bedwyr Lewis Jones (Swansea: Christopher Davies, 1988)
Blwyddyn yn Llŷn (Caernarfon: Gwasg Gwynedd, 1990)
ABC Neb, ed. Jason Walford Davies (Caernarfon: Gwasg Gwynedd, 1995)
Autobiographies, trans. Jason Walford Davies (London: Dent, 1997). Includes translations of *Neb*, *Blwyddyn yn Llŷn*, *Y Llwybrau Gynt*, and *Hunanladdiad y Llenor*

Books edited

The Batsford Book of Country Verse (London: Batsford, 1961)
The Penguin Book of Religious Verse (Harmondsworth: Penguin, 1963)
Selected Poems of Edward Thomas (London: Faber, 1964)
A Choice of George Herbert's Verse (London: Faber, 1967)
A Choice of Wordsworth's Verse (London: Faber, 1971)

R. S. Thomas: Critical and biographical

The following are sources referred to in the present study, critical studies which amplify points made or studies which the author has found rewarding. A full bibliography of critical studies of R. S. Thomas's writing to 1993 is to be found in John Harris, ed., *A Bibliographical Guide to Twenty-Four Modern Anglo-Welsh Writers.* Subsequent work is listed in the annual bibliographies of *Welsh Writing in English: A Yearbook of Critical Essays* (1995-) and at www.bangor.ac.uk/rsthomas.

Agenda 36.2 (1998). Special issue on R. S. Thomas.

Anstey, Sandra, ed., *Critical Writings on R. S. Thomas* (Bridgend: Seren, new ed. 1995).

Astley, Ben. 'Somewhere between faith and doubt': R. S. Thomas and the Poetry of Faith Deconstructed', *Welsh Writing in English: A Yearbook of Critical Essays* 4 (1998), 74–93.

—— 'Iago Prytherch and the Rejection of Western Metaphysics', *Welsh Writing in English: A Yearbook of Critical Essays* 5 (1999), 101–14.

Barker, Simon. *Probing the God-Space: R. S. Thomas's Poetry of Religious Experience* (Ph.D. dissertation, University of Wales, Lampeter, 1991).

Brown, Tony. 'Language, Poetry and Silence: Some Themes in the Poetry of R. S. Thomas', in *The Welsh Connection*, ed. W. M. Tydeman, Llandysul: Gomer, 1987), pp. 159–85.

—— '"Eve's Ruse": Identity and Gender in the Poetry of R. S. Thomas'. *English*, 49.195 (Autumn 2000), 229–50.

Brown, Tony, and M. Wynn Thomas, 'The Problems of Belonging', *Welsh Writing in English*, ed. M. Wynn Thomas. A Guide to Welsh Literature VII (Cardiff: University of Wales Press, 2003), pp. 165–202.

Buuren, M. J. J. van. *Waiting: The Religious Poetry of Ronald Stuart Thomas* (Nijmegen: Katholieke Universitat van Nijmegen, 1993).

Conran, Anthony. *The Cost of Strangeness: Essays on the English Poets of Wales* (Llandysul: Gomer, 1982).

Dafydd, Fflur. '[A] shifting / identity never your own': The uncanny and the unhomely in the Poetry of R. S. Thomas* (Ph.D. dissertation, University of Wales, Bangor, 2004).

David Jones Journal, R. S. Thomas Issue, Summer/Autumn 2001: 99.

Davies, Damian Walford, ed. *Echoes to the Amen: Essays after R. S. Thomas* (Cardiff: University of Wales Press, 2003).

Davies, Grahame. 'Resident Aliens: R. S. Thomas and the Anti-Modern Movement', *Welsh Writing in English: A Yearbook of Critical Essays* 7 (2001–2), 50–77. (A summation of his reading of R. S. Thomas in *Sefyll yn y Bwlch: R. S. Thomas, Saunders Lewis, T. S. Eliot, a Simone Weil*. Caerdydd: Gwasg Prifysgol Cymru, 2000.)

Davies, Jason Walford. *Gororau'r Iaith: R. S. Thomas a'r Traddodiad Llenyddol Cymraeg*. (Caerdydd: Gwasg Prifysgol Cymru, 2003).

Davis, William V., ed. *Miraculous Simplicity: Essays on R. S. Thomas*. (Fayetteville: University of Arkansas Press, 1993).

Dyson, A. E. *Yeats, Eliot and R. S. Thomas: Riding the Echo* (London: Macmillan, 1981).

Humfrey, Belinda. 'The gap in the hedge: R. S. Thomas's Emblem Poetry', *Anglo-Welsh Review* 26 (1977), 49–57.

Lethbridge, J. B. 'R. S. Thomas talks to J. B. Lethbridge'. *Anglo-Welsh Review* 74 (1983), 36–56.

Lloyd, David. 'Making It New: R. S. Thomas and William Carlos Williams', *Welsh Writing in English: A Yearbook of Critical Essays* 8 (2003), 121–40.

Merchant, W. Moelwyn. *R. S. Thomas.* Writers of Wales (University of Wales Press, rev. ed. 1989).

New Welsh Review 20 (Spring 1993). Special 80th birthday issue.

Morgan, Christopher. *R. S. Thomas: Identity, Environment and Deity.* (Manchester: Manchester University Press, 2003).

Phillips, Dewi Z. *R. S. Thomas: Poet of the Hidden God* (London: Macmillan, 1986).

Poetry Wales 7.4 (1972). Special issue on R. S. Thomas, including text of John Ormond's documentary.

Prys-Williams, Barbara. *Twentieth-Century Autobiography* (Cardiff: University of Wales Press, 2004), pp. 120–47.

Shepherd, Elaine. *R. S. Thomas: Conceding an Absence: Images of God Explored* (London: Macmillan, 1996).

Thomas, M., Wynn. *Internal Difference: Twentieth-Century Writing in Wales* (Cardiff: University of Wales Press, 1992).

—— ed. *The Page's Drift: R. S. Thomas at Eighty* (Bridgend: Seren, 1993).

—— 'R. S. Thomas: War Poet', *Welsh Writing in English: A Yearbook of Critical Essays* 2 (1996), 82–97.

Thomas, Ned. 'R. S. Thomas: The Question about Technology', *Planet* 92 (April/May 1992), 54–60.

Thomas, Ned and John Barnie. 'Probings: an interview with R. S. Thomas'. *Planet* 80 (April/May 1990), 28–52.

Ward, John Powell. *The Poetry of R. S. Thomas* (Bridgend: Seren, 2001). Expanded and up-dated edition.

Wintle, Justin. *Furious Interiors: Wales, R. S. Thomas and God* (London: Harper Collins, 1996).

Index